ALL ACTIVITY

FROM THIS MANUAL MUST B

DIMENSION

Y

AND YOUR COPY

OF THIS MANUAL SHOULD REMAIN

STORED IN DIMENSION Z

AT ALL TIMES.

UNAUTHORIZED OR UNSKILLED USE

OF THIS MANUAL WILL RESULT IN THE COMPLETE

DISRUPTION

OF ALL PHYSICAL LAWS GOVERNING THE TARGET PLANET. DO NOT ATTEMPT

ANY

WORLD OPERATIONS WITHOUT THE FULL SUPPORT

OF YOUR NEAREST SCHWA CORPORATION OUTLET. THE UNSANCTIONED MANIPULATION OF PLANETS ALREADY SELECTED BY

THE SCHWA CORPORATION

WILL RESULT IN THE TERMINATION OF YOUR POSITION IN THE SCHWA CORPORATION.

AS ALWAYS, YOUR COOPERATION IS WELCOMED.

BEGIN.

CHRONICLE BOOKS · SAN FRANCISCO

SCHWA ®

WORLD OPERATIONS MANUAL

TRIM

TRIM AND BURN SECRETLY BEFORE CONTINUING.

PRINTED IN HONG KONG. LIBRARY OF CONGRESS CATALOGING-IN-PUBLICATION DATA AVAILABLE. ISBN 0-8118-1585-4. DISTRIBUTED IN CANADA BY RAINCOAST BOOKS, 8680 CAMBIE STREET VANCOUVER, B.C., V6P 6M9. CHRONICLE BOOKS, 85 SECOND STREET, SAN FRANCISCO, CA 94105. www.chronbooks.com NO PART OF THIS MANUAL MAY BE REPRODUCED IN ANY FORM WITHOUT WRITTEN PERMISSION FROM THE PUBLISHER.

NOTICE:

THE CONTENT OF THIS MANUAL IS KNOWN TO CAUSE

EXTREME CONFUSION

IN THE UNINCORPORATED MINDS OF FUTURE SCHWA EMPLOYEES. THE SCHWA CORPORATION IS NOT CONCERNED WITH AND IN NO WAY CAN BE HELD LIABLE FOR THE

COMPLETE REORGANIZATION

OF THE READER'S BRAIN THAT WILL OCCUR IF THIS MANUAL IS READ WITHOUT FULL TECHNICAL SUPPORT FROM DIVISION ÆØ‰

CONTENTS:

INSTRUCTIONS:

Don't follow instructions. Suspect instructions. They are something to be wary of. They will write instructions when they want you to do something. They want you to do what they want you to do. Instructions are broken down in small steps. When you make small steps, you become a smaller person. When you become smaller, you need instructions to tell you where to go and what to do. Those who give you instructions are not doing anything. They are instructing you so you can do something for them. Suspect instructions. They are something to be wary of. Instructions are very detailed and leave nothing to chance. Serendipity is the enemy of the narrow and the organized. Random behavior leads to irregularities. Breakdowns in the system lead to chaos and confusion. If everyone is confused, they will have to write many, many more instructions. Don't follow instructions. Instructions are something to be wary of. If you follow instructions, you cannot do the things you want to do. You do other things instead, the things other people tell you to do. When you only listen to others, you cannot speak. Your ideas are trapped behind the door you helped close. You become the instructions. They will not have to write any more instructions for you, because you will have reached the end of their instructions. Don't follow instructions. Suspect instructions.

UTILIZE

HOW TO GAIN CONTROL

KEEP REALITY SECRET

SCHWA® PLANETARY INVOICE

WORLD OPERATIONS MANUAL

This invoice permits the bearer, _____ to operate as Planet Operator for the planet described. This document should not be taken as an admission of liability by Schwa or its subsidiaries.* For more information about this document, consult The Schwa Corporation's Legal Document ß¥øµ39, "Rights, Responsibilities and Regulations Attached to Planetary Invoices."

TARGET PLANET: _____ PLACE/TIME: _____

PERCENTAGE: _____ PAYMENTS: _____ DUE: _____

* EXCEPT FOR THE LIMITED WARRANTY OF THE MEDIA BEARING THIS INVOICE, THIS PLANET IS PROVIDED "AS-IS" AND THE SCHWA CORPORATION GRANTS NO OTHER WARRANTIES, EXPRESS OR IMPLIED, BY OFFICIAL POLICY OR OTHERWISE, REGARDING THE PLANET AND RELATED ITEMS, THEIR FITNESS FOR ANY PURPOSE, THEIR QUALITY, THEIR MERCHANTABILITY, OR OTHERWISE. THE LIABILITY OF THE SCHWA CORPORATION UNDER THE WARRANTY SET FORTH ABOVE SHALL BE LIMITED TO THE AMOUNT PAID BY THE CUSTOMER FOR THE APPLICATION FOR THIS INVOICE. IN NO EVENT SHALL THE SCHWA CORPORATION BE LIABLE FOR ANY SPECIAL, CONSEQUENTIAL, OR OTHER DAMAGES FOR BREACH OF SAID WARRANTY. THE SCHWA CORPORATION WILL PROVIDE NO SEMINAR EXPLAINING THE ABOVE NON-WARRANTY, AND WILL REIMBURSE NO RELATED TRAINING. IF YOU DO NOT UNDERSTAND THE ABOVE, ACT HOWEVER YOU WISH. DO NOT ATTEMPT TO TRANSFER THIS INVOICE TO ANY OTHER PERSON OR INSTITUTION. IN THE EVENT THAT TRIBUTE PAYMENTS ARE NOT MADE AS DESCRIBED, AN INTEREST RATE OF 26% PER DIMENSION SHALL APPLY. IN SUCH CASE AS THE CLIENT IS UNABLE TO COMPLY WITH THESE TERMS, THE SCHWA CORPORATION RESERVES THE RIGHT TO REPOSSESS THE ABOVE DESCRIBED PLANET BY ANY MEANS NECESSARY UP TO AND INCLUDING MEDIA INUNDATION.

Before we describe the basic procedure for population massage and manipulation, it is extremely important that we pause and do a quick inventory. In order to proceed, please ensure you possess all of the following:

- One (1) Schwa World Operations Manual, in Dimension Y.
- One (1) Schwa Planetary Invoice.
- One (1) Target Planet, listed on the invoice, with a stickperson population.

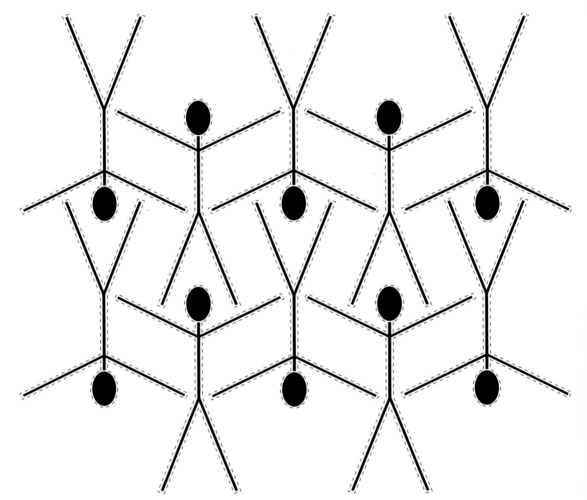

THE SAMPLE STICKPERSON POPULATION: Copy this page as many times as needed then carefully trim out and save these model stickpeople. As you proceed through this manual, use them to test your ideas or to vent your frustrations upon.

MANIPULATING CONTROL

Now that you have verified your inventory, please take a minute to examine the figure on this page, which explains The Unified Dimension Theory in a graphical way. While not explicitly necessary to gain manipulative control, it forms the basis for Schwa's Mythic Structure and is thus useful as an initial indoctrination.

The root commands needed to properly control stickpeople, both on an individual and planet-wide basis, should become clear to you after studying both The Unified

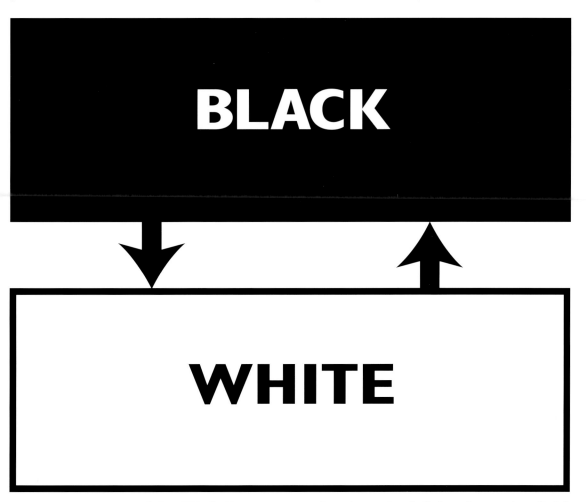

THE UNIFIED DIMENSION THEORY: Proven to be the sole defining factor in all 26 dimensions, this theory accounts for all perceived phenomenon. It has also been shown that any conceptions made beyond this are merely reiterations of the theory.

Dimension Theory and Mythic Structure schemata. In large part, the following chapters only elaborate on the two. As an additional study aid, this edition of The World Operations Manual now features a helpful diagram of stickperson perception. As you can see, stickperson internals are quite simple; their perceptions are limited to a seven-address bank of archetypical registers.

Given this primitive apparatus, The Schwa Mythic Structure is extremely robust. Multilayered enough to hide Schwa intentions from the unprepared, it still avoids the operating problems associated with complex structures. It derives most of its power from The Good/Bad Logic Trap built into the target stickpeople. In a nutshell, this

THE BASIC MYTHIC STRUCTURE FOR ALL SCHWA PLANETS: Without question this is the most critical structure in your effort to gain control. Use of this mythic structure has been proven to be 100% effective, for obvious reasons.

structure describes an awe for our powerful operatives (good or bad) combined with and opposed to a powerful xenophobia. When confronted with a suitable manifestation, the target stickperson (whether singly or in groups) is paralyzed by its inability to choose between two courses of action, i.e. kill or worship. A third option is created on the spot; the target isolates the incident, denies its reality, and instantly creates an industrial-strength smokescreen for Schwa initiatives.

Now that you have a basic foundation from which to view all world operations, take the time to thoroughly and patiently go through each of the following chapters, taking care to adapt the procedures outlined to your particular planet. Remember, have fun!

DIAGRAM OF THE PERCEPTION OF THE STICKPERSON: The interior of the stickperson has been found to contain an amazing array of perceptions, all of which can be easily manipulated to further The Corporation's consolidation of control.

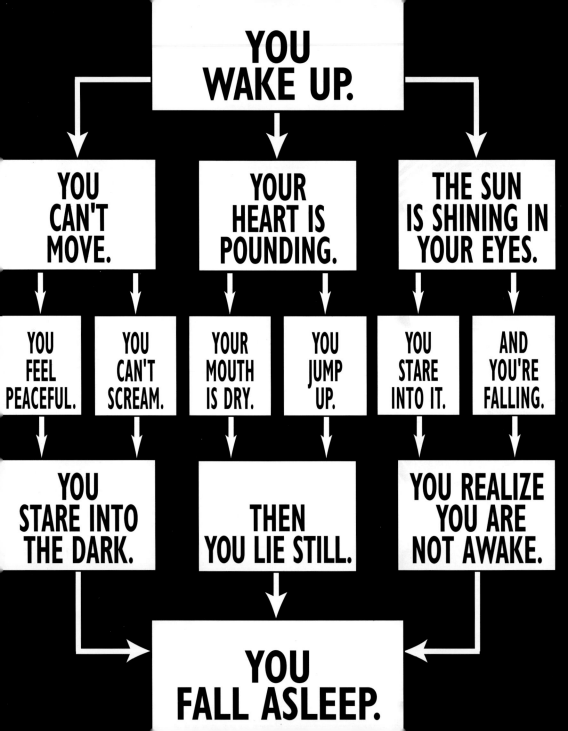

ACTUALIZE
HOW TO COMMUNICATE

CREATE
OUTRAGED VICTIMS OF
INJUSTICE

ACTUALIZE-SECTION 2: DIMENSIONS B & Y
SUBTLE SIGNALING METHODS

In Schwa's experience, the most efficient path to total planet domination lies in persuasion. Brute-force approaches, while attractive by virtue of their speed, must be maintained over an indefinite period and can thus consume a virtually infinite amount of resources simply to hold on to past gains. Stickpeople must not only be persuaded to accept Schwa's total control, they should be conditioned to ask for it by name. This approach obviously places a high emphasis on communication. The Operators' first instinct is to place their emphasis on those media with a high signal-to-energy ratio, but the first subject we will cover is the field of direct corporate communications and signage. All Schwa-to-stickpeople transactions are built on these primary conduits.

Local Schwa representatives will need a number of individual representation artifacts. These objects are both physical assertions of their identity and disposable information containers, and usually both identify the bearer's position and provide contact information. This manual includes several pre-fabricated templates, both for Schwa operatives and employees of the template subsidiaries. Since most target planets manufacture these items using pulp-based technology, the templates are optimized for those methods. However, the templates are overloaded with several subtextual designs, and will thus provide assistance in diverging scenarios.

Corporate correspondence is the second conduit for which this manual provides example material, and in many ways this is the most important item in the section. Whether it travels through physical messengers, pulp-based transmissions or wave-form packeting systems, the essential form of the "business letter" is the same. The idea is to communicate one of three basic messages (demand, investigation or refusal) in a clear and concise way, while also appearing warm and respectful. The included example follows a standard transaction through from first contact to assimilation. It can be extended to conform to local practices, and the content is readily adaptable to various transmission technologies.

Since Schwa or its subsidiaries will usually have to establish and maintain some sort of physical presence on the target planet, the final examples of this section deal with large-scale signage in its various forms. It is recommended that Operators think beyond the obvious usage in marking components of the operations' infrastructure. Large-scale messaging systems are an important part of every persuasive campaign of subjugation, and can be very effective for a certain range of transmissions. When their presence corresponds with a corridor of travel, they reach the stickperson during a highly tedious phase, when they are craving some sort of distraction.

Greeting

Sales

SALESPERSON

<NAME>
<Contact Information>

Proposition

Old Tyme

Moderne

Sample Business and Calling Cards: Insert relevant information and fold or mutilate, as required. See also Section 7.

SCHWA®

FROM: OPERATIONS DEPARTMENT

To: <Target Corporation/Government/Organization>
<Location>

<Salutation> <Name>,

This letter is to inform you that you have been selected to take part in Schwa's new March of Advancement initiative. We would like for you to review the enclosed materials and information kit, which we believe you will find both exciting and educational. We here at Schwa believe that cooperation is the best way to achieve our goals, and we're willing to invest all of our resources to ensure that both our organizations can enjoy the fruits of partnership.

Thank you in advance,
<Operator's Local Name> <Operator's Local Title>

P.S.: Just sign and return the simple contract in The Information Kit and it's onward to advancement!

SCHWA®

FROM: OPERATIONS DEPARTMENT

To: <Target Corporation/Government/Organization>
<Location>

<Salutation> <Name>,

You may have noticed several changes since you've joined us as a March of Advancement member. Chief among them, of course, is your new subsidiary status-- I'm sure I don't have to tell you about the enhanced prestige your organization has enjoyed, now that you are part of the Schwa organization. But don't thank us, thank yourself-- only you could have made this possible, by your far-sighted and selfless action when you joined our initiative. Your example has helped us sign up even more organizations as dedicated as yourself.

Unfortunately, as our family of pioneers has grown, so has the job of keeping this program healthy and robust. The monthly payments to The March of Advancement steering committee will have to increase, as per the attached financial statements and invoice.

Your Advancement Leader,
<Operator's Local Name>
Operator's Local Title>

Sample Form Letters: For use in corporate correspondence. Insert applicable information and attack.

SCHWA ®

FROM: OPERATIONS DEPARTMENT

To: <Target Corporation/Government/Organization>
<Location>

<Salutation> <Name>,

No one is more disappointed than we are that your organization has been unable to make the monthly payments to the Steering Committee. We wish there was something we could do to improve this situation, but it seems we are left with no choice. As per the March of Advancement agreement, we hereby inform you that we are proceeding with The Asset Seizure, as per the enclosed documents.

Rest assured that there will forever be a place for you in our organization. After you have undergone the required Loss Counseling (see attachment), feel free to report to our Assignment Department for your new cubicle.

Your Leader,

<Operator's Local Name> <Operator's Local Title>

SCHWA ®

FROM: OPERATIONS DEPARTMENT

To: <Target Corporation/Government/Organization>
<Location>

<Name>,

You and all evidence of <Target Corporation/Government/Organization> have been terminated and/or eliminated.

<Operator's Local Name> <Operator's Local Title>

LIFE IS MORE FUN IF YOU DON'T TALK

ALONE CANNOT YOU IT RESIST.
SCHWA

THE POSSIBILITIES AREN'T CDI ENDLESS. INDUSTRIES

Sample Billboards: Use for primitive signage, or enhance with available local technology.

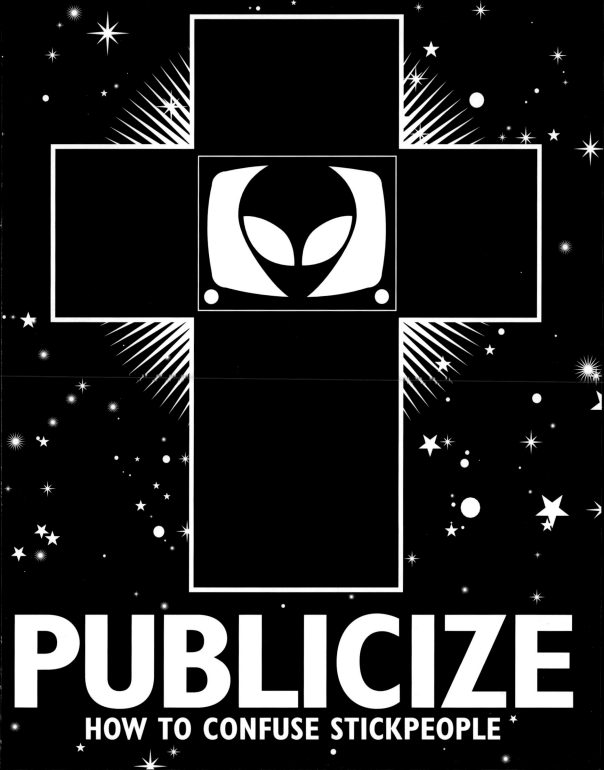

PUBLICIZE

HOW TO CONFUSE STICKPEOPLE

IGNORE ALL INFORMATION

ON CREATING INFORMATION

With very few exceptions, **Schwa's** targeted planets are riddled with **existing** mass media structures. It is usually easier for Schwa's local **operatives** to manipulate existing media than it is to build such delivery systems from scratch. (For a notable exception, **see the** Schwa Dimensional Archive Item ŒÒ° "Media Enrichment: **Surreptitious** Media **Introduction** Over Several Local Generations"). The astounding similarities encountered in these media structures can be explained **by** the strong herding instinct in the dominant stickpeople of the **Schwa** target planets. Most **of** the populations interesting from Schwa's standpoint have only recently, or barely, evolved from **primitive** grazing creatures. This also explains the effectiveness of **images containing** healthy fields of the stickpeoples' favorite plant **material**, accompanied by favorable weather conditions **and**, in the case of carbon-based stickpeople, water.

Media manipulation campaigns are **crucial** to the success of any Schwa world operation. A well-controlled and managed media **structure** will save a great deal of time and energy, and also allow **for a greater** margin of error in every aspect of the **manipulation** This section will concentrate on the "high-yield" channels **of** mass communication: These channels are the oldest and, usually, **the most trusted.** Frequently pulp-based, they tend to be static and primarily analog in their **production**, although there have been cases **of** fully digital deliveries, and even one or two planets where **direct** brain communication was the only channel that realistically fell into the **high-yield** category. Since 91 percent of the targeted planets contain visual and static high-yield channels, the **bulk** of this chapter's **weapons** are designed for such channels.

Past experiences have helped us come up **with** a number of robust slogans which, if properly used as campaign kernels, will achieve **the maximum** amount of psychological pliability. A key point to remember is that high-yield media are best used as a platform from which to **launch** a concentrated **assault on** the planet's electronic media. Campaigns such as The **Schwa** Channel's "Export Television Slavery" and "TVs Are Needles" **are** perfect illustrations of this approach. Of course, many **successful** planetary manipulations have relied almost exclusively on low-yield campaigns, but it is usually safer, career-wise, for **the Planetary Operator** to avoid such outdated and irregular approaches. If the standard strategy produces results **deviating from** the norm, a Media Squad will be dispatched to assist in bringing **the project** back on track.

The initial stages of the penetration are modest, small-scale **and cryptic**. The choice of the base of **operations** is crucial: If the population center is too large, the Operator **risks early exposure.** If the population center is too small, access to the means of dissemination may be **troublesome** and conspicuous. But these are **logistical** issues, best covered in Dimensional Archive Item Âƒ¥. Past initial-stage **efforts** have involved the heavy use of keychains and stickers. While these approaches **are** still valid in some cases, it is **important** to remember that a product line, where applicable, is a far more efficient place to start. **If the target** audience **is** conditioned early on **to accept the** transactional, rather than the subscriptional, model, each successive step toward **ultimate** ownership will be that much easier. The product line also requires far less **effort to conceal** the ultimate **motivations**: Its graphics-intensive objectification contrasts sharply with the communications-intensive nature of the written word or ideogram. With the graphics-intensive approach kept in mind, this edition of The World Operations Manual features The Emergency Schwa Cartoon Kit. Not only does this kit provide a template of proven cartoon images, but it can also be used as a backup production environment in case your primary production facilities are lost or damaged.

The "Export Television Slavery" campaign is illustrated using a sample of clothing bearing the slogan itself. Though venerable, this broadcast technique is a requirement for any planetary manipulation involving stickpeople who do in fact wear clothing. Although the broadcast area itself is modest, the payload reverberates within the affected brain units with an effectiveness only rivaled by wave form delivery systems. When counted alongside its primary usefulness as the first step toward mandatory planetwide uniforms, and the ability to mark each wearer with tracking devices, the humble shirt or hat may become the beachhead of your entire operation.

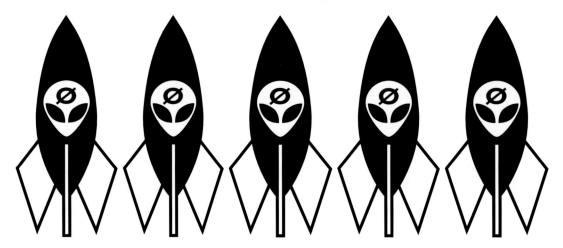

EXPORT TELEVISION SLAVERY

THIS T-SHIRT DESIGN SHOULD BE THE CENTRAL ELEMENT IN YOUR MEDIA CAMPAIGN. ENLARGE AND TRANSFER ONTO AS MANY SHIRTS AS YOU CAN. YOU MAY MAKE ONE FOR YOURSELF.

EXPORT TELEVISION SLAVERY

MFHYIRHDKGFLKSKRTSDHGJDSJKFBIOPSWLSJDGWERWUDFJTGUDJSDHWYGHM
VNCGDYWTQEEITPYLHKVNMNHFVDSXGJFTIUGHFHDGDGDCHCHVBMNBKMNLHP
GFGOFUDTDSERWWQDASFDHFUGJHVHCVJFIGKUKUBMBNVHFHFGRYRYTHGUFY
FGCTGFHGFHFHFUGGHGHFYDTCXFXZCSEDWTRUTYIUPOIPJLJKHJNBMBNCVBDF
GDGDGFHFWQDASFDHFUGJHVHCVJFIGKUKUBMBNV

THE SCHWA CHANNEL™

WATCH IT TONIGHT!

MFHYIRHDKGFLKSKRTSDHGJDSJKFBIOPW
LSJDGWERWUDFJTGUDJSDHWYGHMVNC
GDYWTQEEITPYLHKVNMNHFVDSXGJFTIU
GHFHDGDGDCHCHVBMNBKMNLHPGFGO

THE SCHWA CHANNEL™

TRIM AND USE THESE ADVERTISEMENTS IN YOUR PUBLICATIONS.

Insert copy appropriate to your objectives.

TVs ARE NEEDLES.

MFHYIRHDKGFLKSKRTSDHGJDSJKFBIOPSWLSJDGWERWUDFJTGUDJSDHWYGHMVNCGDYWTQEEITPYLHKVNMNHFVDSXGJFTIUGHFHD
GDGDCHCHVBMNBKMNLHPGFGOFUDTDSERWWQDASFDHFUGJHVHCVJFIGKUKUBMBNVHFHFGRYRYTHGUFYFGCTGFHGFHFHFUGGHG
HFYDTCXFXZCSEDWTRUTYIUPOIPJLJKHJNBMBNCVBDFGDGDGFHFWQDASFDHFUGJHVHCVJFIGKUKUBMBNV

THE SCHWA CHANNEL™

WATCH IT TONIGHT!

PRESS RELEASE CONSTRUCTION

Instructions for the Excitement-Enhanced Schwa Press Release Construction Set:

The latest Schwa Press Release Construction Set (PRCS) is a complete upgrade from previous versions and emphasizes the new component-based approach to planetary persuasive techniques. It has also been integrated with PlanetStat's built-in reporting tools, allowing the Operator to coordinate all public relations output with the target stickpeople's gullibility and acceptance readings instantaneously.

The function of the new PRCS is similar to previous versions, with the following major changes:

• All Power Verbs now auto-tense; it is not necessary to explicitly invoke the Tensor. Invocation of the Tensor will have no effects on tensed Power Verbs.

• The Handy Phrase Units are fully adjustable and adapt well to a wide range of sentence environments.

Complete instructions for the use of the PRCS can be found in Primary Library Document µ®z, "The Schwa Press Release Construction Set Reference Manual," but new users may find the following "Quick Start" section easier to use in an emergency.

QUICK START:

STEP 1: Select an introductory sentence from the "Beginnings" menu. Tailor the selection to the product or service you would like to introduce or emphasize to your target stickpeople. For example, if you intend to manipulate local planets for amusement purposes, a good introductory sentence would be "In the most ambitious effort in history..." You can change the introductory sentence at any time simply by selecting another introductory sentence from the "Beginnings" menu. (Go to Step 2)

STEP 2: Select an applicable object from either the "Atomic Noun" or "Handy Phrase Unit" menu. By convention, the object should summarize the message of the release, although there are no technical reasons for doing so. (If you have chosen an Atomic Noun, go to Step 3A. If you have chosen a Handy Phrase Unit, go to Step 3B)

STEP 3A: If the Atomic Noun you have just placed is blinking red, you need to add a Targeted Adjective. Select an applicable simple descriptor from the "Targeted Adjective" menu. If the Atomic Noun you have just placed is blinking green, it requires a Handy Phrase Unit. Select an appropriate complex descriptor from the "Handy Phrase Unit" Menu. (If the Atomic Noun is not blinking, go to Step 4)

STEP 3B: If the Handy Phrase Unit you have just placed is blinking red, you must add an Atomic Noun. Select an object from the "Atomic Noun" menu and go to Step 3A. (If the Handy Phrase Unit is not blinking, go to Step 4)

STEP 4: Congratulations! You have successfully completed your introductory sentence! (Go to Step 5)

STEP 5: Activate the Paragraph Filler. You may be prompted to answer several questions as the Paragraph Filler parses your introductory sentence and completes the introductory paragraph. If the completed paragraph is not satisfactory, you bring up the Paragraph Properties window and use the numerical sliders to adjust grammar, style, tone and brightness. (Go to Step 6)

STEP 6: Select several Handy Phrase Units from the "Handy Phrase Unit" menu and begin the Phrasal Junction Coordinator. Once the phrases have been coordinated, follow the instructions in Step 7.

STEP 7: If the Handy Phrase Unit you have just placed is blinking red, you must add an Atomic Noun. Select an object from the "Atomic Noun" menu and go to Step 8. (If the Handy Phrase Unit is not blinking, go to Step 9)

STEP 8: If the Atomic Noun you have just placed is blinking red, you need to add a Targeted Adjective. Select an applicable simple descriptor from the "Targeted Adjective" menu. If the Atomic Noun you have just placed is blinking green, it requires a Handy Phrase Unit. Select an appropriate complex descriptor from the "Handy Phrase Unit" Menu.

(If the Atomic Noun is not blinking, go to Step 9)

STEP 9: Congratulations! You have just completed an opening sentence for an internal paragraph. To fill the paragraph, go to Step 5.

BEGINNINGS

The Schwa Corporation is proud to announce...

In the most ambitious effort in history, The Schwa Corporation will...

Today The Schwa Corporation brings stickpeople one step closer to...

In an attempt to further consolidate its planet share, Schwa has...

HANDY PHRASE UNITS

with no purchase necessary

with a speedier and more accurate psychological interface

at no additional charge

while supplies last

for a limited time only

the culmination of years of development

a turnkey solution

for all your (adjective) needs

Schwa research efforts

as part of this amazing offer

instant consciousness retrieval from any Schwa terminal

featuring a user-friendly hierarchical power structure

bring about the first artificial lunar eclipse

ATOMIC NOUNS

system target subject consumer units happiness rollout package component Schwa See also: (Pre-fab Slogan) (Official Product) (Meaningless Scientific Unit)

TARGETED ADJECTIVES/ADVERBS

advanced   powerful   planetary   central
non-habit forming   technological   Schwa
emotional   subatomic   orderly   blissful
key   auto-tensing   auto-detect   capable
defense   component

AUTO-TENSING POWER VERBS

introduce   target   deliver   command
supply   announce

PRE-FABRICATED SLOGANS

Scared Yet Not Afraid
We Wanted the Future, We Have It.
Start Living Forever Today

OFFICIAL PRODUCTS

Inflatable Stickperson Decoy

Fact and Truth Preservative
Universal Time Clock
Cold Fusion Cooler
26 Dimensional Telescope
Psychic Pain Remover
Universal Knowledge Pak
Reincarnation Counter
Temporary Existence Reliever
Atomic Sex Enhancer

MEANINGLESS SCIENTIFIC UNITS

only 7.5 times the inodal waste
371,293 CPH verified
39 percent increase in output
.052 Lost-Bounce Ratio
110% overachievement per second

INCHOATEINCOHERENTINFORMATION
INCHOATEINCOHERENTINFORMATION
INCHOATEINCOHERENTINFORMATION
INCHOATEINCOHERENTINFORMATION
INCHOATEINCOHERENTINFORMATION
INCHOATEINCOHERENTINFORMATION
INCHOATEINCOHERENTINFORMATION
INCHOATIMAGINEAWORLDDORMATION
INCHOAWITHOUTINDUSTRYORMATION
INCHOATEINCOHERENTINFORMATION
INCHOATEINCOHERENTINFORMATION
INCHOATEINCOHERENTINFORM TIO

SERMONIZE

HOW TO BROADCAST

TRANSMITTING IMAGE

Although the power of planet-wide or regional broadcast networks are immediately obvious to even the most casual observer, many Operators never seek to integrate them into their plans for domination until later stages. Broadcast power comes at a significant price in time and resources, and it frequently seems more economical to message-saturate target populations through older and cheaper delivery systems. But the high-yield benefit of broadcasting should not be postponed until the need for it has passed. Its power should be harnessed at an early stage, so that its use can result in an exponential acceleration of the psychological subjugation necessary for later stages of domination.

Structurally, the prime advantage of broadcasting is its built-in hierarchy. The transmission emanates from a single, technically superior source, and the targets of the broadcast are made quite lowly in comparison. Response is practically impossible, and the targets are aware that they are but a small part of the mass audience. Pulp-based media may share a similar model, but the target's experience is usually a solitary one, creating an artificial impression that they are the sole beneficiary of the transmission. Since static media are freed from the strict time-indexing of broadcast channels, that impression occasionally may even be correct.

Of secondary but functional importance is the low skill level required to experience a broadcast. While static media tend to require a certain level of literacy, and at the very least stimulate the target's imagination, most broadcast channels make no such demands. Moreover, during most broadcasts, the capacity for critical thought tends to shrink. Its imagery is explicit and fast-paced, allowing no time for lengthy explorations of any sort. The thrust of any successful broadcast invariably tends toward entertainment of some kind. On the whole, its character fulfills propaganda needs so well that it is surprising to see it used for any other purpose.

Using broadcast channels does not actually require outright control, or even secret influence. Most planetary networks are ravenous for any new movement or idea, since they quickly use and exhaust existing entertainment opportunities. A few catchy slogans, a suitably graphic pictograph and several staged events are the basic building blocks for a low-cost broadcasting campaign that will pay dividends in later stages of the operation. Care must be taken to keep the superficial content and style of the events fresh; although networks are easily entertained and manipulated, they are also easily bored.

This chapter's materials are designed to aid in the manipulation of existing networks, before an explicit (or implicit) assimilation, or for the creation of a Schwa-controlled planet-wide network.

THE *SCHWA* CHANNEL ™
TELEVISION
PROGRAM

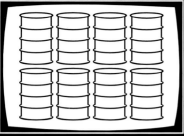

HOST: OUR PLANET HAS ALL THE RESOURCES IT CAN STORE...

SOUND: CARS STARTING

HOST: ...AND OUR PLANET IS FULL OF POWERFUL INSTITUTIONS...

SOUND: PHONES RINGING

HOST: ...THIS PLANET HAS MILLIONS OF WEAPONS OF INCREDIBLE STRENGTH...

SOUND: WHITE NOISE

HOST: ...AND ITS CAPITAL RESERVE IS BEYOND CALCULATION...

SOUND: RAIN FALLING

HOST: ...BUT A PLANET NEEDS TO HAVE SOMETHING MORE THAN ALL THAT TO BE TRULY GREAT.

SOUND: WIND

HOST: WHAT CAN WE DO THAT WILL MAKE US NEVER FORGET HOW GREAT THIS PLANET IS?

SOUND: HURRICANE

HOST: SEE A SPECTACLE BEYOND ANYTHING WE HAVE EVER SEEN OR CONCEIVED OF BEFORE...

SOUND: TIDAL WAVE

HOST: ...BROUGHT TO OUR MOON BY THE SCHWA CORPORATION, FOR YOUR EDIFICATION...

SOUND: EARTHQUAKE

HOST: ...THE MOON BLAST! SEE IT HAPPEN LIVE ON THE MOON THE NIGHT OF _____

SOUND: THUNDER

SCRIPT FOR RADIO/TELEVISION

The following is an example of the type of event that can be staged, whether the actual events are occurring or not. This is intended to serve as a guideline only, you will want to create scenarios and events suited to the unique circumstances of your planet. Use your imagination, you may be surprised at the results of even the smallest efforts.

THE SURPRISE ANNOUNCEMENT

(music up, music fades, medium shot on **HOST**)

HOST: Good evening and welcome to The _____ Talk Show, I'm _____ (smiles) and I'm here this evening broadcasting to you from Media Central. We're talking with _____, the new CEO of the Schwa Corporation, who has just been elected Owner of this planet. We want to find out what direction our planet will be going in terms of the universal community. Well, _____, we know that the...

ACTOR/CEO: You are required to call me CEO _____ .

HOST: Yes, CEO _____... I, I apologize. I didn't intend to imply that we are friends. I know that you are reviled, I mean revered, by all the inhabitants of this planet. We'd like to know: what do you intend for us in the coming millennia?

ACTOR/CEO: Thank you _____, thank you for bringing me on your show. First of all (turns to camera), Stickpeople of this planet, you must each give The Schwa Corporation one half of your earnings daily or we will have you destroyed by our corporate facilitators.

HOST: O.K., O.K., we know that it's really important we participate in the universal community as willing contributors. What do you intend to do with the meager funds that we will be providing to you?

ACTOR/CEO: First of all, We plan on opening up more casinos across this universe, and, Stickpeople of this planet, I've talked to the aliens and they're kind of stupid, all right? People think they built the ancient monuments of this world... (shakes his head no), they're really dumb. So, here goes: Schwa Casinos... I can see it now. We'll be raking in the space-bucks, raking in the space-bucks (waves hands). We plan on elevating this planet to the level where all it's resources will be turned into manufactured products. I mean ALL of it's resources, every ounce of rock, water and air. But it starts with the casinos.

HOST: Will these casinos be open to all inhabitants of this planet?

ACTOR/CEO: Oh yes, definitely. First of all, we plan on going to the nearest moon...

HOST: Will the stickpeople of this planet be allowed to go there?

ACTOR/CEO: Definitely! We're going to dump all of the money from what used to be this planet's economy into this, we're going to take the entire output, and what we're going to do is hook-up this fun-run shuttle kind of thing. We're going to fly to the moon, which right now, is under construction as the first Schwa Casino. We'll be hollowing out the center of the moon and making a "virtual universe" inside. And, we'll be running the shuttles daily, the Schwa Shuttle will be flying every day.

HOST: Well, this is fascinating, CEO _____ ! And, I really hope (smiles) that I can remain on your good side and that you will continue to frequent our...

ACTOR/CEO: All it takes is your money, really.

HOST: We hope that you will continue to frequent our show and keep us posted. We'd like to be your exclusive publicity slash propaganda network.

ACTOR/CEO: We do want you to know that although we plan on enslaving the entire population of this planet, do not take it personally, because... you know, The Schwa Corporation is now the legal owner of this planet...

HOST: O.K., CEO _____, we have to wrap this up. Thank you all very much for watching/listening and join us next week when we will have... um, I really don't know who we're going to have...

ACTOR/CEO: (sticks his face into the camera) Blah blah blah.

HOST: Have a good night from Media Central! (looks off-camera) Oh, I see. O.K., well, actually next week, we will be having CEO _____'s assistant, Treasurer _____ of The Schwa Corporation.

ACTOR/CEO: (laughs) We're planning on taking control over all the other planets in this system right away...

HOST: Yes, well, I see we're out of...

(music comes up, fade to black)

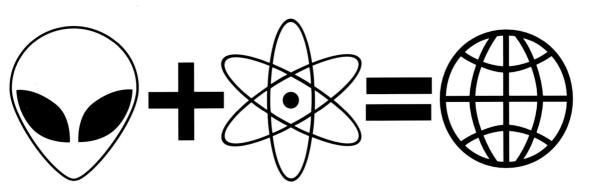

HALLUCINATION IS A REALITY
REALITY IS A HALLUCINATION
HALLUCINATION IS REALITY A
REALITY IS HALLUCINATION A
A HALLUCINATION IS REALITY
A REALITY IS HALLUCINATION
IS REALITY A HALLUCINATION
IS HALLUCINATION A REALITY
HALLUCINATION REALITY IS A
REALITY HALLUCINATION IS A
A IS HALLUCINATION REALITY
A IS REALITY HALLUCINATION
IS HALLUCINATION REALITY A
IS REALITY HALLUCINATION A
IS A REALION HALLUCINALITY
IR SEALINATINY A HALLUCION?

ORGANIZE
HOW TO MAKE EVERYONE WORK

STOP DOMESTICATING YOURSELF

DISCOVERING PRODUCTIVITY

Once your stickpeople have been reprogrammed to accept only Schwa-originated lexical tokens, it can be safely assumed that the bulk of the preprocessing is done. At this point it is wise to invoke the services of the nearest Schwa Psycho-Verification unit in order to authenticate the required level of cultural sterilization. But this is a minor detail, and a far more important task awaits: That of organizing your now-docile population into an efficient production force. This chapter is meant as an introduction to basic social algorithms, and will include some discussion of the latest trend toward a more efficient component-based population organization.

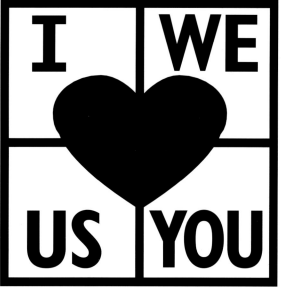

THIS IMAGE IS KNOWN TO CONTAIN IMAGES WHICH YOUR STICKPEOPLE WILL FIND IRRESISTIBLE. SPRINKLE THIS ICON LIBERALLY THROUGHOUT YOUR WORK PROGRAMS AND FORGE IT INTO PRODUCTS.

The oldest, but not necessarily most efficient, organizational structure is, of course, The Big Stickperson Hierarchy. Descended from primitive tribal structures common to nearly all stickpeople, the modern version is enhanced by an artificial cult of personality made all-pervasive through the use of various mass media. You have the choice of casting yourself as the smiling, parent-like figure, or you may employ the services of an especially gullible local puppet. A third option is The Schwa Virtual Dictator, created just for this purpose. Although it is not available in the basic World Operations Tool Kit, Schwa is still looking for testing sites.

No discussion of social engineering would be complete without religion, and it makes for a very robust solution, since most situations involve a large installed base of spiritually oriented stickpeople. Schwa Theocracies do well on technology-poor planets, where massive visual spectacles (the trivial task of slamming a comet into a nearby moon, for example) are usually all that is needed to display what they would consider a godlike power. This scenario allows The Operator some special freedoms. A Big Stickperson must appear in the flesh with a certain regularity, and the associated mass media campaign never truly ends. In a theocratic situation, The Operator need not even maintain

I FEEL GOOD.

I FEEL BAD.

I FEEL NOTHING.

I FEEL GOOD.

I FEEL NOTHING.

I FEEL BAD.

I FEEL NOTHING.

I FEEL GOOD.

I FEEL GOOD.

I FEEL BAD.

I FEEL NOTHING.

I FEEL NOTHING.

I FEEL GOOD.

a fixed manifestation, but can throw any sufficiently advanced pyrotechnics at the population, as long as the visual metaphor is accompanied by supplemental text.

More recently, a popular alternative to both The Theocracy and The Big Stickperson Hierarchy has developed as Planet, Inc. Indeed, rumors suggest that Schwa eventually wants to migrate all its existing subsidiaries to this model. Essentially Schwa writ small, this template involves replacing all existing cultural structures with corporate departments. It is part of the trend toward component-based management, since individual departments can be quickly substituted across multiple hierarchies. Although this structure shows great promise, its shortcomings lie in its relative inefficiency. Most stickpeople, being only slightly more evolved herd animals, lack the level of sophistication necessary to operate bureaucracies. Operators find they must spend a large part of their time adjusting small portions of the structure.

Where production capacity and sheer power is the primary objective, the most fitting solution is usually found in an Induced Duality. This hybrid consists of two artificially separated organizations locked in a titanic cultural and political struggle. The organizations can be any mix of the three mentioned so far, or a patchwork of existing corporate structures. This powerful system has several advantages; its setup time is blazingly fast and the opposition creates a tension strong enough to propel stickpeople-output to the highest levels ever recorded. The artificial animosity is enough to raise average stickperson output by 65 percent over any other system. This template must be seen as a short-term solution, however. Control over such forces are difficult to maintain, and a rampant Induced Duality quickly self-destructs in one of two ways. The intense production either depletes the planet's natural resources, or the competition erupts into mutual destruction.

These initial templates are the building blocks to the later Schwa World. Their low entertainment value is offset further into the process of planetary conquest, and many other chapters discuss ways to inject mindless, random entertainment into your planet.

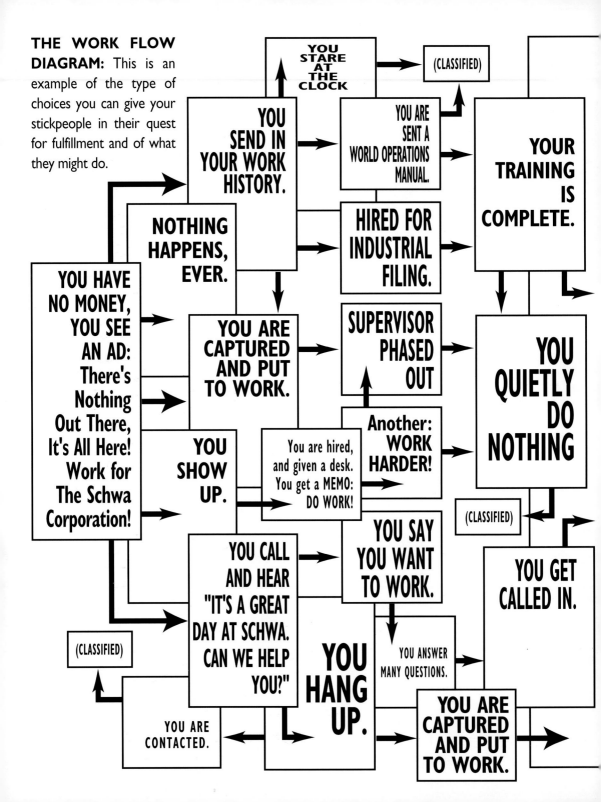

THE WORK FLOW DIAGRAM: This is an example of the type of choices you can give your stickpeople in their quest for fulfillment and of what they might do.

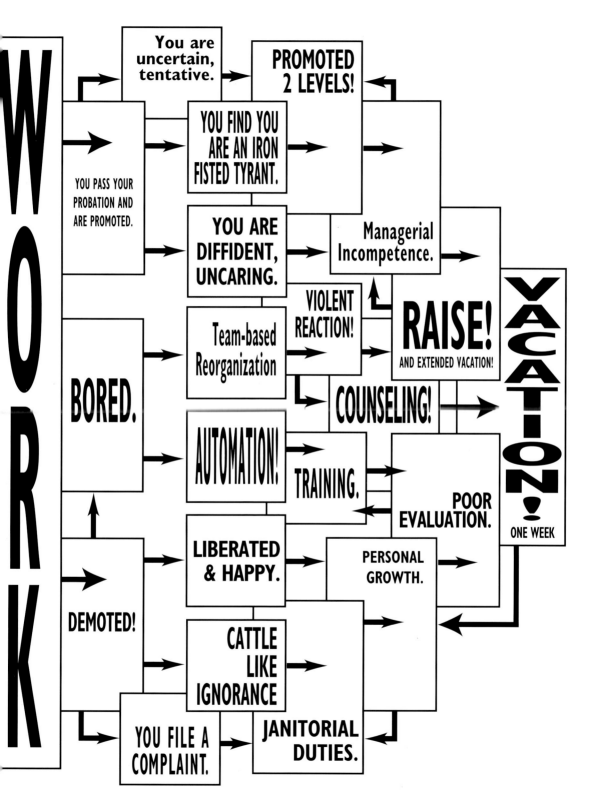

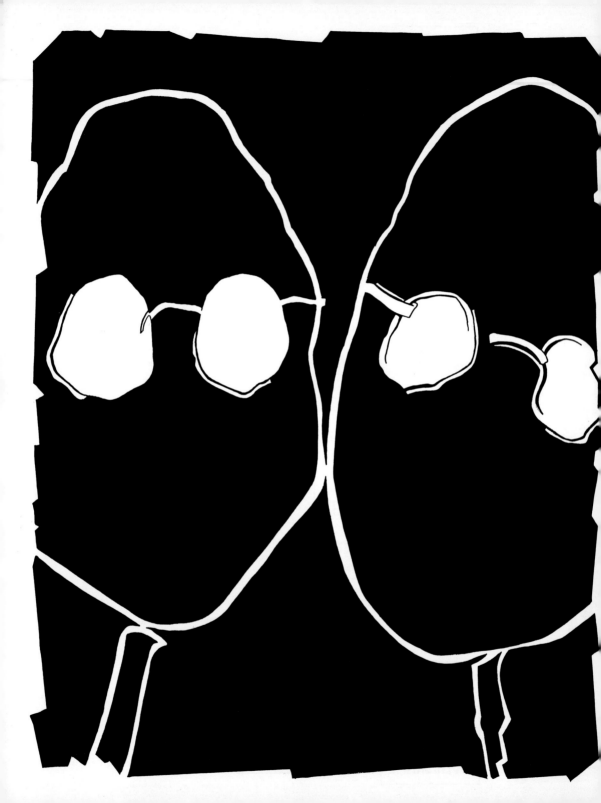

SUBSIDIZE
HOW TO ACQUIRE MONEY

SUBSIDIZE-SECTION 6: DIMENSIONS F & U
ACCESSING STORED EFFORT

A Schwa planet cannot live on efficiency and promotion **alone**. Resources must be acquired **and exploited by** using the most aggressive and practical method possible, preferably within the framework of **a** Type Å13 abstracted-unit-based, **capital-oriented** economic system. Target stickpopulations are usually chosen with this in mind, but an Operator should always be prepared to wean a **planet** off such primitive economic relationships as barter, **communal altruism** and lottery-based resource allocations.

The reason Type Å13 **systems lend themselves so well to** Schwa operations lies in **the** strong cleavage between the political and economic sectors. Absent the customary **political control of the means of production**, the Operator need not complete a socio-political takeover before initiating economic

THIS LICENSE MUST BE POSTED IN A CONSPICUOUS PLACE

BUSINESS LICENSE

Ⓢ

LICENSE NUMBER

13

EFFECTIVE TIME/PLACE:
BUSINESS CLASSIFICATION:
BUSINESS LOCATION:

NAME OF BUSINESS:

EXPIRATION TIME/PLACE:
TOTAL FEE PAID:

NOT VALID UNLESS CERTIFIED FOR THE FULL AMOUNT OF THE LICENSE. LICENSED BUSINESS TO BE CONDUCTED IN CONFORMITY WITH AND SUBJECT TO THE PROVISIONS OF THE ORDINANCES OF THE LAWS OF THE REGION THIS LICENSE IS IN. THIS LICENSE EXPIRES AS SPECIFIED ABOVE.

OFFICIAL LOOKING SIGNATURE

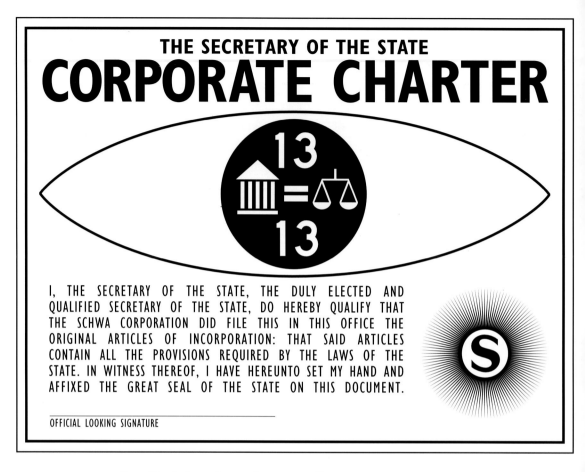

maneuvers. The **individual-oriented** system of managed competition allows The Operator to pursue a **cost-efficient** divide-and-conquer strategy that ultimately will be interpreted by the target stickpeople as the result of **natural economic system** processes.

This section **offers** example documents designed to allow The Operator to manipulate **the most** common institutions and regulations associated with Type Å13 systems. Included among the various governmental and contractual instruments is The Schwa Stock Certificate, which is specially designed to **alter** its content upon authorized voice command. Although other Schwa-to-stickpeople **documents** are **similarly** equipped, The Stock Certificate is unique in that its fuzzy-logic neural net is equipped **to make the necessary adjustments** without requiring Operator-preset contents.

The other documents included should be fairly **straightforward**. Given the wide variation in local economic custom, some or **all will have to be**

extensively adjusted before their usage becomes practical. In some cases, the Operator will have to **improvise** instruments to suit the local conditions. Although these procedures are well-documented in Dimensional Archive Item Ò̂Î ("2001 Economic Tricks for Primitive Worlds"), the following guidelines may prove useful:

• Remember that a stickperson's capacity for understanding decreases as the number of lexical tokens increases. Twist the syntax and add tokens beyond what is necessary for simple obfuscations.

• In a similar vein, use contracts both recursively and sequentially: Use contracts to make contracts which make the initial contracts. The end result is that the Operator is given the dominant position.

• Use large bureaucratic organizations to trap hostile elements and slow any possible counterattacks. Red tape, if liberally dispensed, is a powerful tactical weapon.

Number

_____ Shares

Incorporated under
the laws of _____

THE SCHWA CORPORATION®

Capitalization _____ Shares Common Stock at _____ Par Value

This certifies that

_____ is the registered holder of

_____ shares of

The Schwa Corporation

Transferable only on the books of the Corporation by the holder hereof in person or by Attorney upon surrender of this

Certificate properly endorsed. In Witness Whereof, the said Corporation has caused this Certificate to be signed by its duly authorized officer and its Corporate Seal to be hereunto affixed this _____ Place _____ Time _____

_____

SIGNED

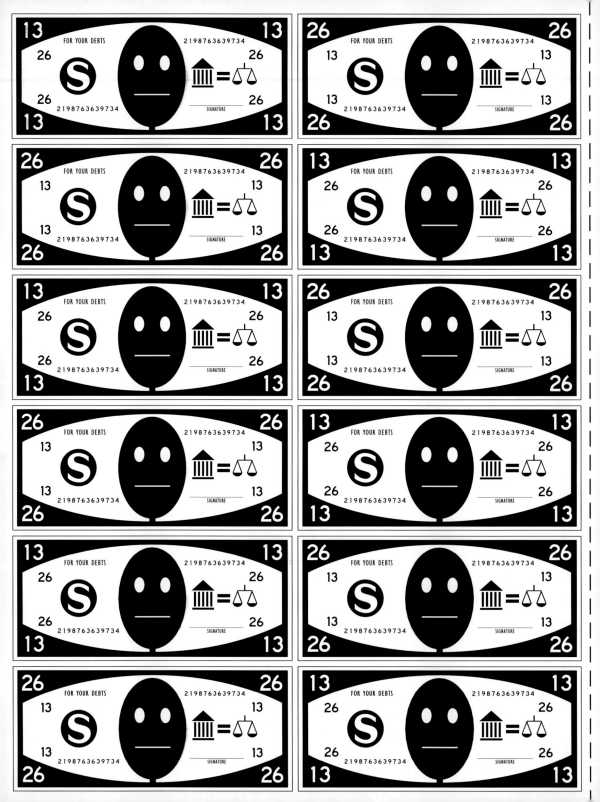

SCHEMATIZE

HOW TO ADVANCE THE PLAN

IT'S COOL
IT'S CRUEL

EXPLORING SUBSIDIARIES

A well-run Schwa Dominance Operation usually assumes the eventual presence of unquestioned love for the Schwa brand name on the part of target stickpeople. Quite frequently, however, an Operator may find such an assumption optimistic. In such cases, it is prudent to operate behind a more or less elaborate front of subsidiaries. The corporate structure can be as complicated as The Operator desires, as long as the trail back to The Schwa Corporation is well-concealed. It is important to remember that the use of subsidiaries is not limited to Schwa-intolerant situations; even on planets where Schwa is preferred, a network of subsidiaries serves many useful functions.

One obvious benefit centers on image-detrimental Operator activities. Subsidiaries make ideal avenues for such actions and will absorb any negative response without affecting The Schwa Corporation's standing within target stickpeople's public translation structures. The obscured and confusing links between The Schwa Corporation and its subsidiaries should be sufficient to isolate culpability. Even where The Operator has already implemented procedures for sub-media actions, subsidiaries can be used to great strategic advantage. In a form of brand-cannibalization they can be pitted against one another to provide large-scale mass entertainment in a spectacular way. They can also be combined and recombined to form an incessant stream of partnership announcements, which both enhances the impression of progress and validates stickpeople herd instincts.

While the construction and maintenance of Schwa subsidiaries is covered in Dimensional Archive Item œåÓ, this section provides two template organizations to use in your operation. The Eldritch Company and CDI Industries are component-based prefabricated corporations designed to seamlessly weld into any Schwa-compatible domination structure. Although the templates can operate individually, they are best optimized for efficiency when they are instituted together. In Schwa tests, their combined energies have shown a 169 percent increase in output over the long run. The following illustrations provide an excellent example of the complexities that are possible in a fully realized combined subsidiary environment.

THE POSSIBILITIES
AREN'T
ENDLESS.

CDI
INDUSTRIES

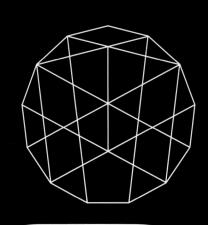

CDI
INDUSTRIES
CENTRAL OFFICE

DO
MORE
NOW

I ♥ US
WE ♥ YOU

S

13

SECURITY
PROVIDED BY
THE ELDRITCH CO.

INDUSTRIES
ADDING INSULT TO INDUSTRY

THE
ELDRIT
COMPA
FACTORY

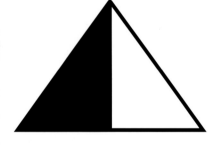

THE SCHWA CORPORATION®

31

I	WE
US	YOU

ALONE CANNOT YOU IT RESIST.

SCHWA

CHOOSE

CHOOSE

A SUBSIDIARY OF CDI INDUSTRIES

VIDEO SURVEILLANCE
THE ELDRITCH CO.

62

DO MORE NOW

PERSONALIZE

HOW TO MAINTAIN SUCCESS

SHOP BY PILL

PLEASURABLE CONSUMPTION

Once a firm Schwa-oriented dominance pattern has been established, The Operator's job has only just begun. At this stage in the operation, complacency is the greatest threat to Schwa's success; In order to be comfortable in their brand new world, your subjects must be entertained with a constant stream of consumables. The bulk of these will consist of artifacts designed to discreetly weaken and disrupt critical-thinking patterns, but this section will also introduce a template rational belief system-- The Schwa Corporation Psychograph-- which strongly categorizes individual stickpeople into Schwa-compatible personality types while maintaining the illusion that they are in control of their own destiny. One of the first artifacts which should be introduced to Schwa's new subjects is The Instant Stickperson Decoy. This product's purpose is twofold. Primarily, it manufactures an unknown anxiety while also addressing it; buyers of the product are made to worry about the unknown while Schwa simultaneously casts itself as the buyer's ally. The deeper effect of the product is to condition subject stickpeople to accept the idea of their own individuality as a product. Once this concept has been established, traditional antipathy to psychological retrofitting never becomes an issue. The Emergency Personal Defense Product is similar in configuration. Like The Decoy, The EPDP is a cheap answer to a vague question. At no point does it actually make the buyer feel safe; the unknown threat it assumes into existence generates so much fear that even an effective product would be insufficient to dispel the consumer's anxiety. Its instructional pattern is stronger and somewhat more overt, and thus targets the algorithmically sensitive areas of stickpeople psychology.

We have previously discussed the usefulness of Schwa-branded clothing in preparing stickpeople for control structures. Bracelets and other markers are quite closely related, and present the additional advantage of being more overtly associated with ownership. Bracelets can quite easily be converted from evidence of elite early adoption to a general symbol of subordination. As an added bonus, bracelets and other such items support a large and complicated hierarchical structure, simply by arranging ink or symbols in a trivial way. The Operator need not even try to hide tracking technology; any obvious component on the bracelet will usually be interpreted as a status symbol.

Schwa places great emphasis on conditioning techniques that demonstrate a high degree of self-replication. These psychological harvesting campaigns are quite self-sufficient and ruthlessly effective over the long run, and replace the need for a large network of support staff.

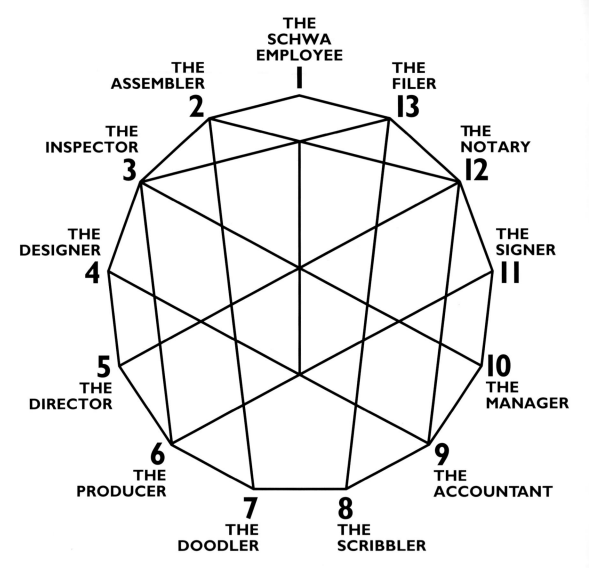

The Schwa Corporation Psychograph: Use this personality typing system to prepare your workforce for Schwa-controlled employment. Include several vague pieces of explanatory text, or simply allow the design to take on a life of its own. While your stickpeople debate its validity and their own relationship to the system, they will condition themselves for assimilation. The chart is sure to create a robust and active subculture upon introduction, with or without supplemental text. The personality types correspond quite closely to the basic Schwa employee types-- an obvious benefit to The Operator faced with the need to retrain an entire planet. Even if the subculture diverges from the original graphic and types, the mere process of personality typing has been shown to decrease task-placement costs by 52 percent.

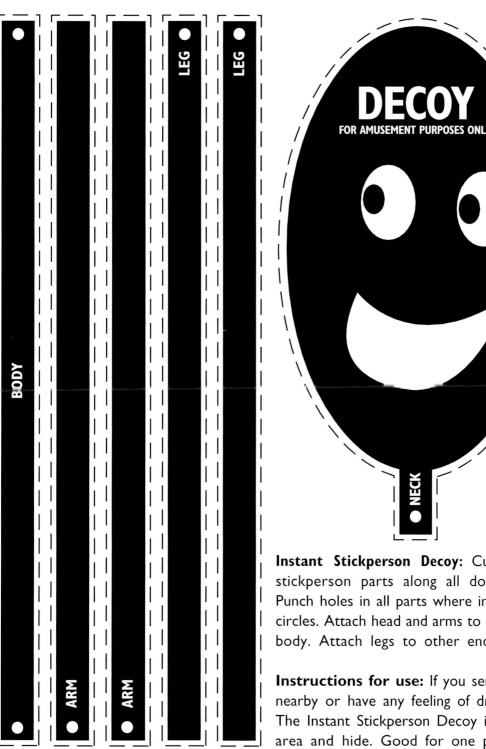

BODY

ARM

ARM

LEG

LEG

NECK

DECOY
FOR AMUSEMENT PURPOSES ONLY

Instant Stickperson Decoy: Cut out the stickperson parts along all dotted lines. Punch holes in all parts where indicated by circles. Attach head and arms to one end of body. Attach legs to other end of body.

Instructions for use: If you sense danger nearby or have any feeling of dread, leave The Instant Stickperson Decoy in an open area and hide. Good for one panic only.

TRIM

SCHWA

SCHWA

2: FOLD DOWN & OUT, BOTH SIDES.

3: FOLD DOWN & OUT, BOTH SIDES.

1: FOLD IN HALF, BLACK SIDE IN.

PRODUCT WARNING: THIS IS NOT A TOY AND SHOULD ONLY BE MANUFACTURED BY AN ADULT UNDER ADULT SUPERVISION. THROWN OBJECTS CAN BE EXTREMELY UNPREDICTABLE IN FLIGHT AND CAN IMPACT IN UNWANTED PLACES. POPPING HAZARD: THIS COULD POP SOMETHING. BLINDING ALERT: THIS PRODUCT COULD MOMENTARILY OR PERMANENTLY OBSCURE YOUR VISION. QUALITY NOTE: THIS ITEM MAY IN FACT BE ONLY MARGINALLY AERODYNAMIC.

The Emergency Personal Defense Product: Trim along the black-white border. Follow instructions on The EPDP to assemble. Grasp fuselage between thumb and index finger. Tilt arm back and throw. Pick up EPDP and repeat. Do not throw at anything larger or more powerful than you are, or at any Schwa Representative.

The Schwa Personal Bracelet Set: Be the envy of your peers as you walk down the street wearing one of these stylish Schwa Bracelets. Everyone will see you and know that you belong-- to us, in fact. Fun! Try laminating them!

TRIM

Instructions: Copy & trim bracelets along black-white border. Cut along solitary white dotted line, put bracelet on chosen appendage and cut the white dotted line necessary to ensure proper fit. If you occasionally feel a slight electrical charge, the bracelet is working.

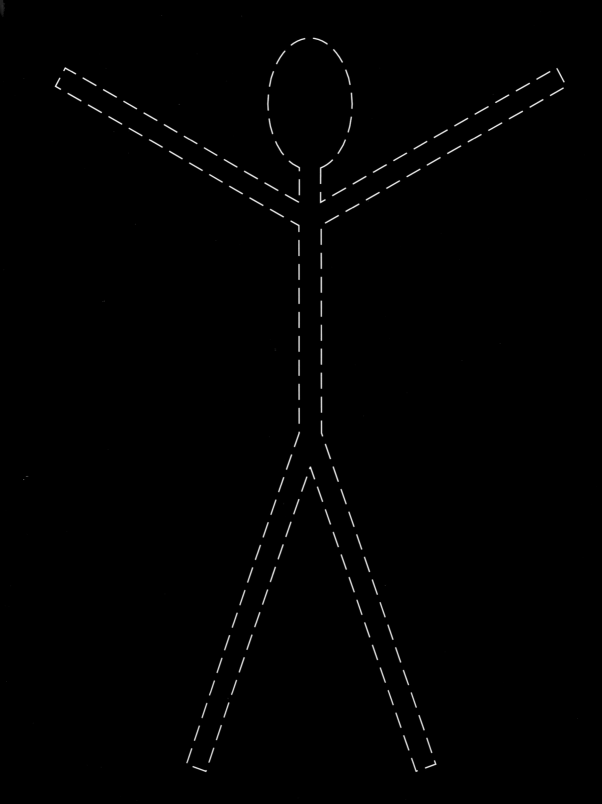

MAXIMIZE

HOW TO EXCEL

THE STRUCTURE IS NO STRUCTURE

OPERATIONS WITH STYLE

In the previous sections, this manual has sought to clarify the issues surrounding planet-oriented control initiatives and present an efficient algorithm for success. Schwa has built its success on its corporate policy. But it will always remain important for individual Operators to adapt specific implementations of the operation to fit local conditions. Although deviation from pre-fabricated schemes always involves the risk of actual work and original thought, the results of creative deviousness can be surprising, and many Operators find this opportunity to improvise quite agreeable.

With that in mind, this final activities chapter is not so much the conclusion to the work sections of The World Operations Manual, but the beginning of advanced training and study. The first step on this path is the classification that allows potential Operators to place themselves in the Schwa taxonomy and identify individual idiosyncrasies through categorization.

The Success Vs. Failure Graphic in this chapter includes both a general classification of the likely readers of this manual and a graph depicting standard distribution curves corresponding to these classifications. It is recommended that each Operator study this information carefully, so that their success curve will more closely approximate Curve M. Bear in mind that Curve M does not actually reach Dimension Z, but approaches it very, very closely. This is a function of the average CEO's will to ambition, which prevents the true CEO from finishing their project so completely that the success of the venture destroys the CEO's wish to express their ambition. In fact, Schwa research has established a direct correlation between early project success and eventual project failure over the long term, a phenomenon most likely related to the difficulty of maintaining interest in such long-term projects as planetary assimilation once early steps have proven successful. For this reason, Schwa recommends that Operators take steps early in the project to both hamper their efforts and dampen initiative-outcomes to prevent domination burnout. For a full treatment of self-sabotage and its special value to large-scale organization-building efforts, consult Dimensional Archive Item −ø˜, "Induced Mediocrity in Planetary Micromanagement."

Another area of further studies involves The Schwa CogNet, a packet network connecting the cognitive apparatus of every stickperson that has ever been in contact with any aspect of Schwa. Nanoscopic indicators and transmitters allow The CogNet to provide real-time measurement of stickpeople motives. Gateways have been placed on applicable planets to The CogNet and provide a stable source of data. A canny Operator will acquaint themselves thoroughly with The CogNet's usage.

WORLD OPERATION SUCCESS VS. FAILURE OUTCOMES GRAPHIC

Ⓐ The Unauthorized: Steals or buys a World Operations Manual and uses it without technical support or supervision.

Ⓑ The Dilettante: Looks at all of the pictures but does not read the text.

Ⓒ The Dreamer: Thinks about getting a World Operations Manual.

Ⓓ The Romantic: Looks through The Manual for aesthetic reasons.

Ⓔ The Drifter: Flips through a Manual randomly at some point.

Ⓕ The Literalist: Has extremely poor language or visualization skills.

Ⓖ The Miracle: A sudden revelation that allows The Literalist to continue.

Ⓗ The Rocket: Shows incredible early success followed by disappearance.

Ⓘ The Loner: One who does not know of The Schwa Corporation.

Ⓙ The Rationalist: Has to believe and have faith in an orderly universe.

Ⓚ The Talker: Questions all aspects of The Manual.

Ⓛ The Artiste: Attempts to elaborate upon The Manual.

Ⓜ The CEO: Is given a sanctioned copy of The World Operations Manual, wisely follows all instructions in order and has technical support with supervision. The True CEO diligently participates in all activities, has an intuitive grasp of ritual mystification and is able to keep a secret. These conditions are always followed by unlimited success.

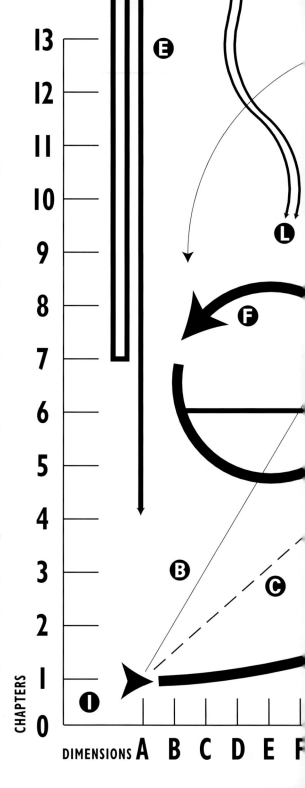

ONLY THROUGH DIRECT EXPERIENCE CAN YOU BECOME VERSED IN THE FINER ASPECTS OF THE SCHWA COGNET. GO TO THE LOCATION INDICATED BELOW AND STUDY IT. NOTE: IF THIS IS A SANCTIONED COPY OF THIS MANUAL, YOU SHOULD BE ABLE TO READ THE SECRET CODEWORD FOR THE SCHWA CORPORATION'S ADVANCED TRAINING CENTER IN THE BLACK BOX BELOW:

http://
www.
theschwacorporation
.com

SYMBOLIZE

AN OVERVIEW

ALIEN EXISTS

UNIFIED DIMENSIONS

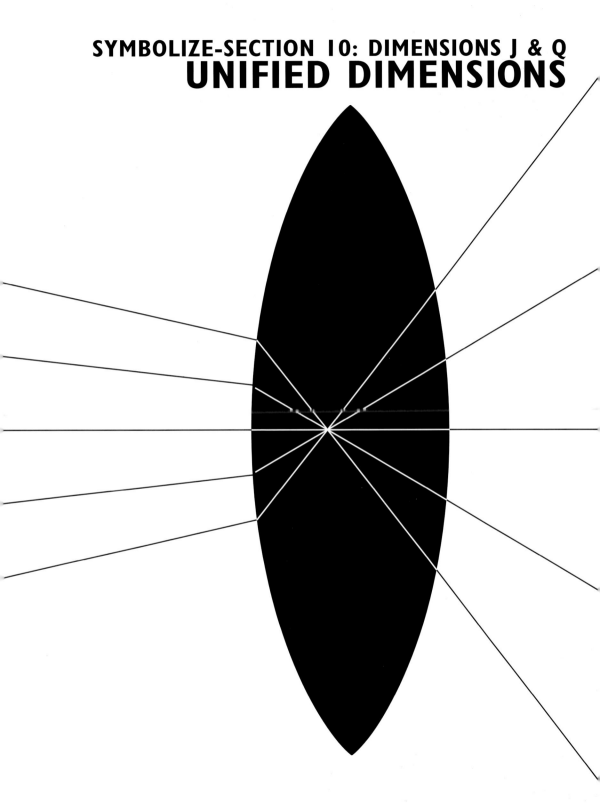

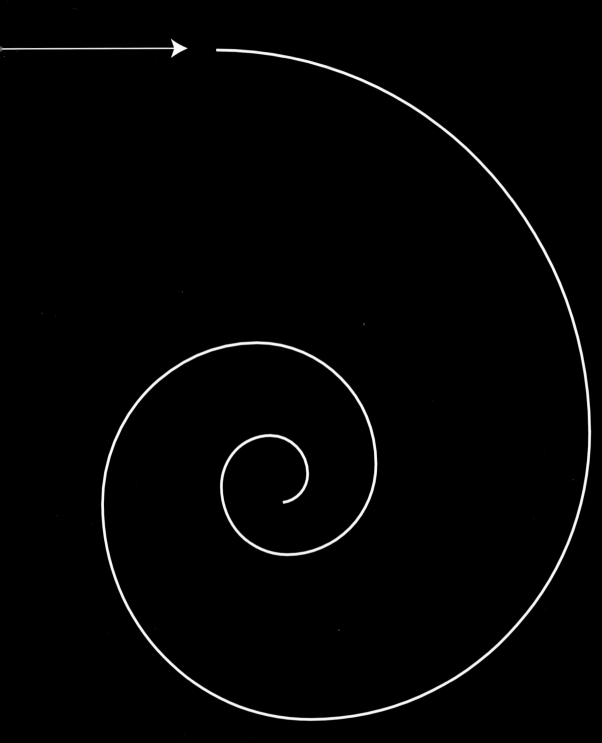

A

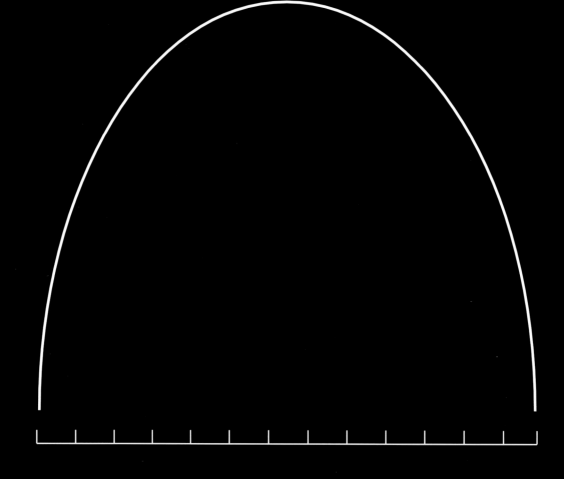

Z

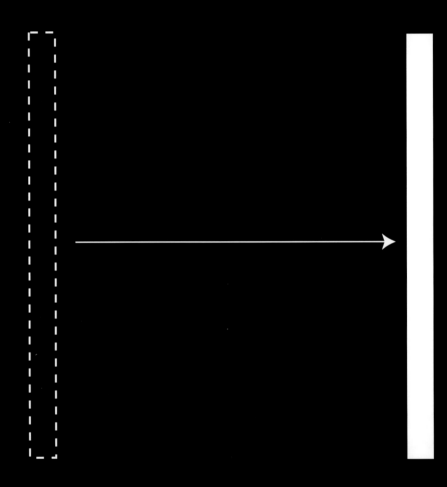

B

Y

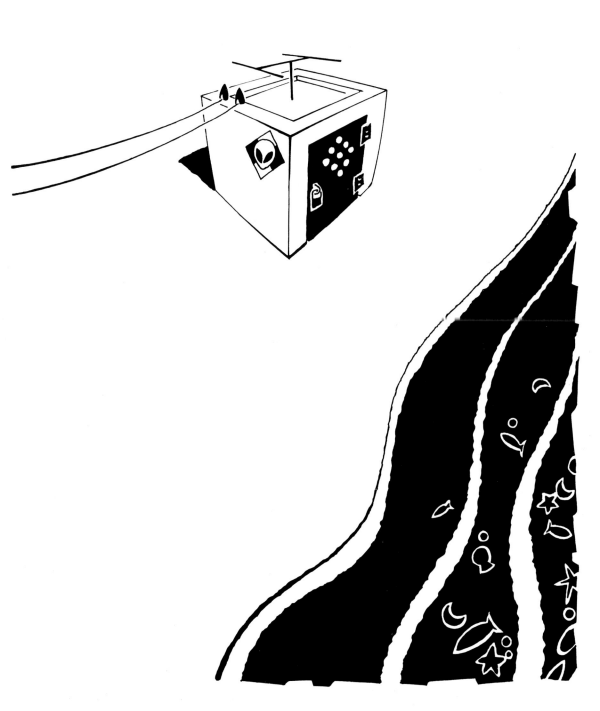

C

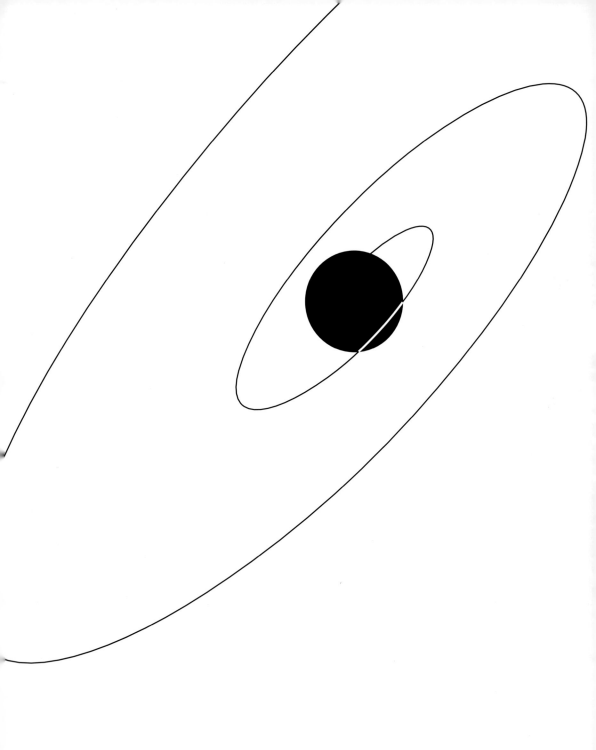

X

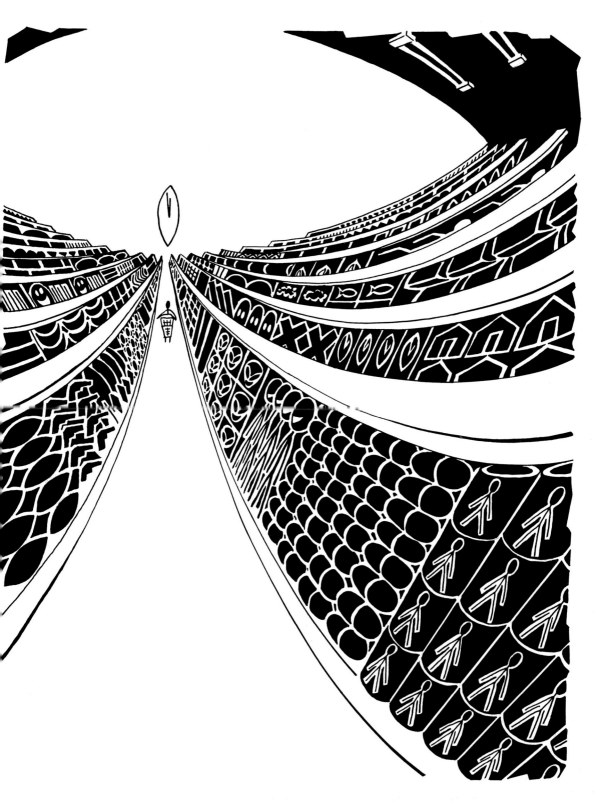

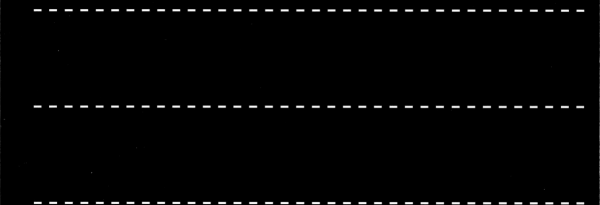

E

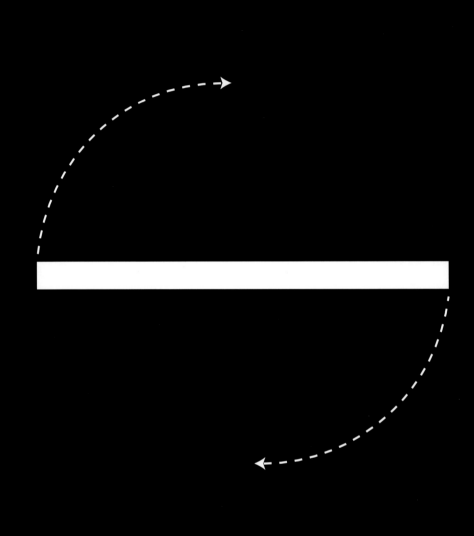

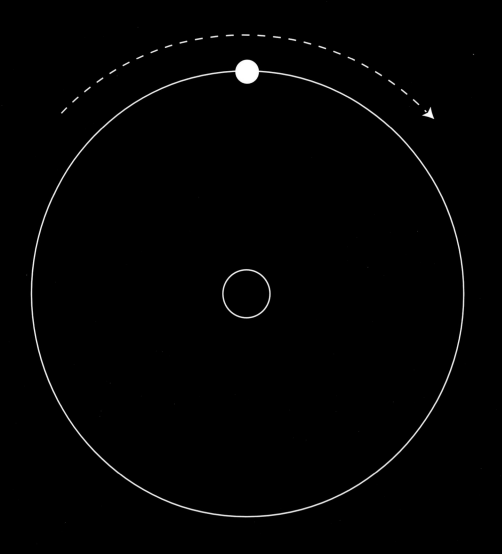

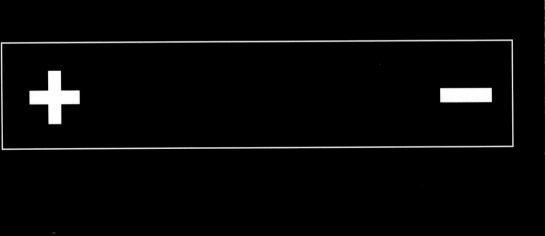

T

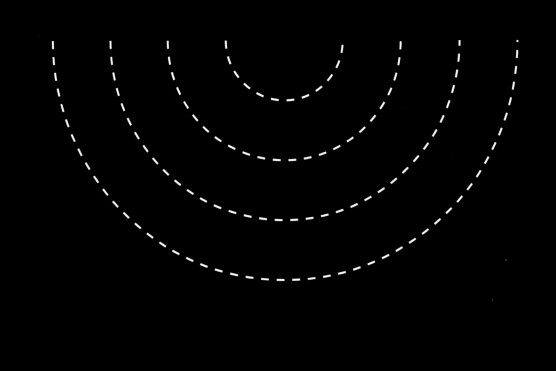

H

S

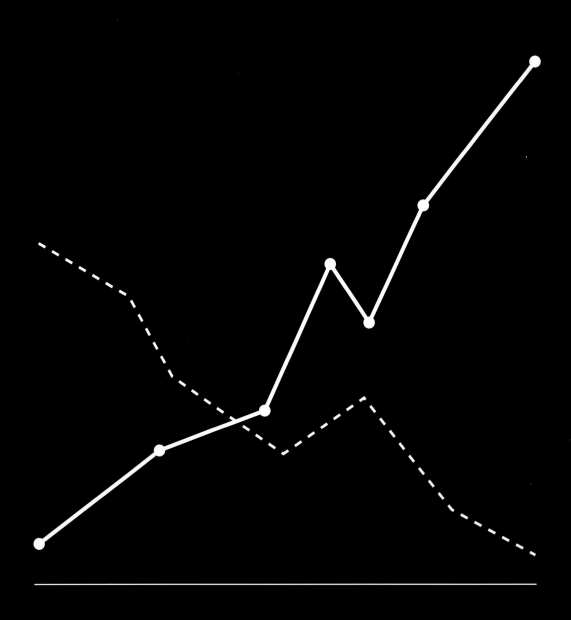

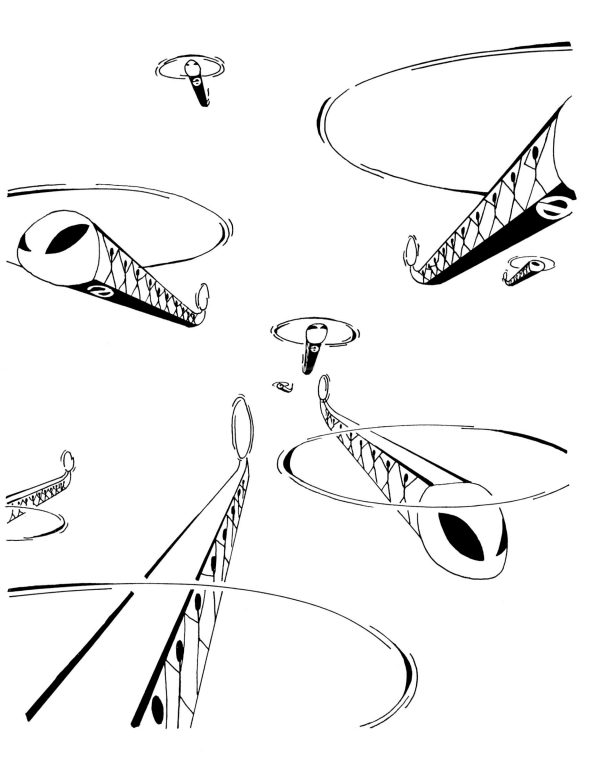

J

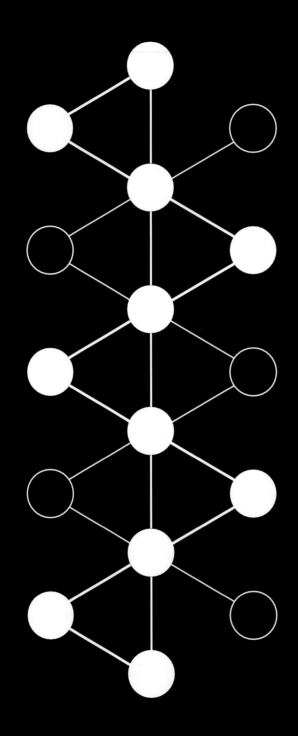

Q

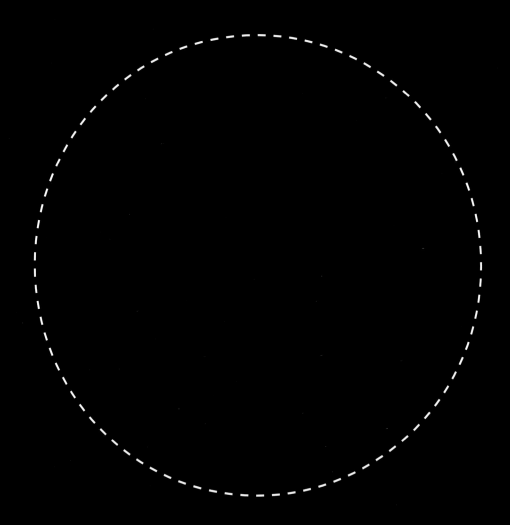

K

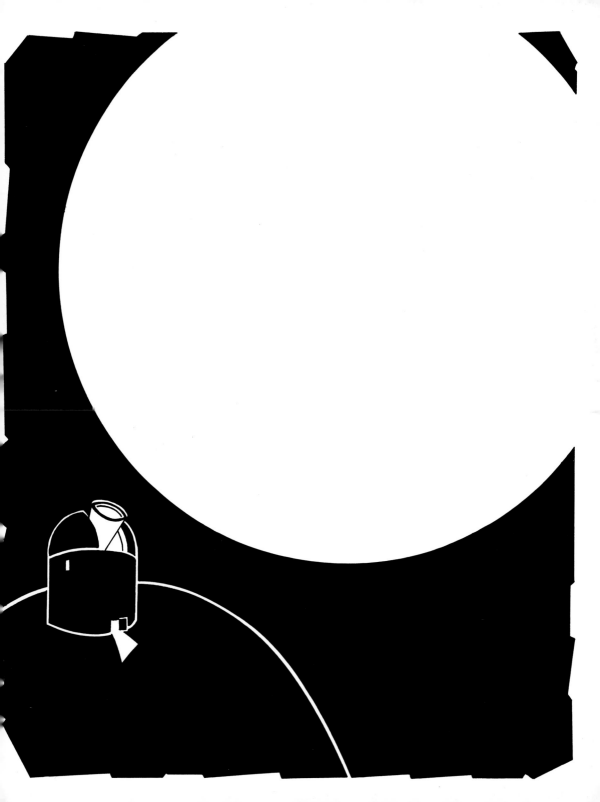

P

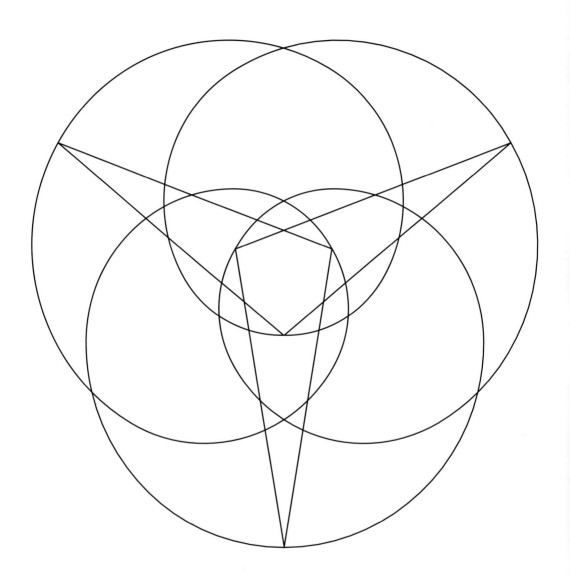

L

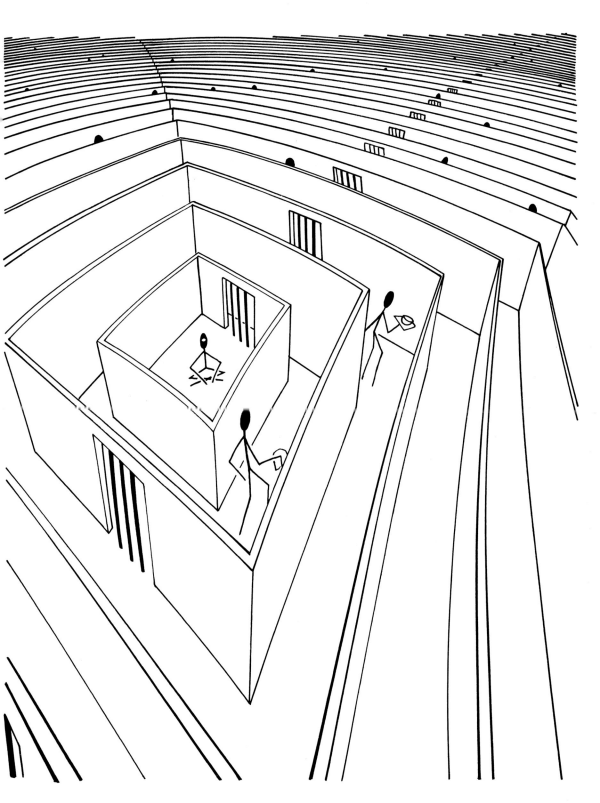

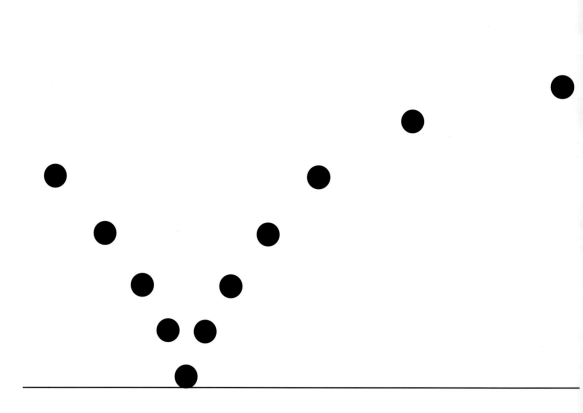

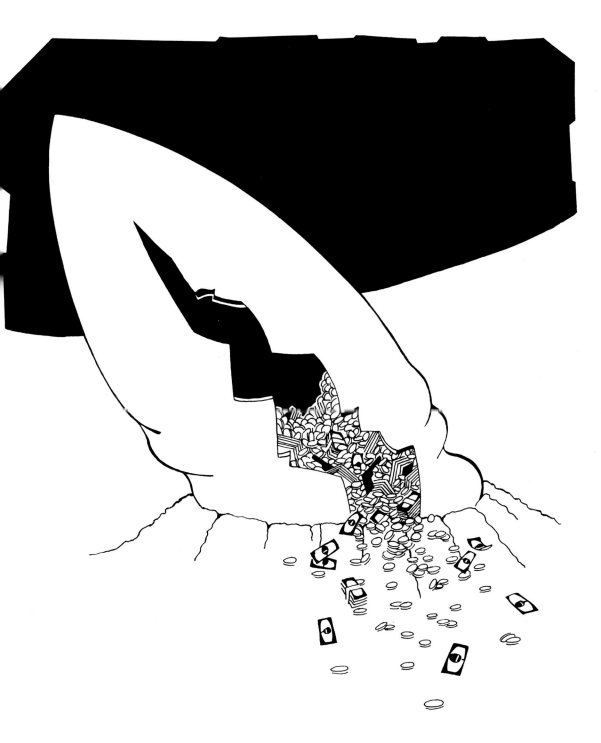

M

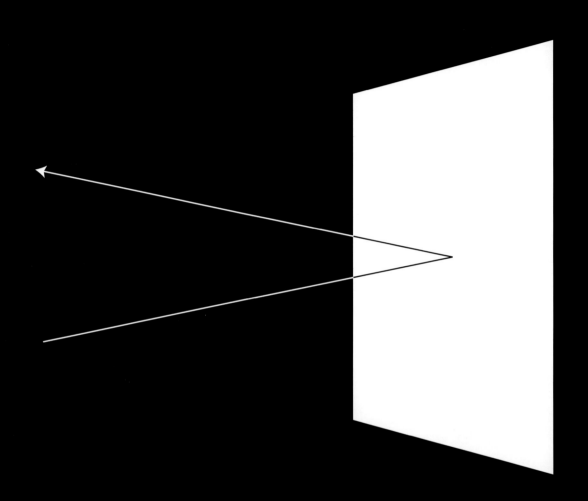

METHODIZE

HOW TO BUILD THE FUTURE

SCIENCE:
100%
IMAGINATION FREE

FUTURE CONSOLIDATION

The beauty of the Schwa plan is that once the initial takeover is completed and the subjects are correctly conditioned, your Schwa world can run itself, provided the right steps are taken early. Experience has shown that the primary challenge facing a newly-created Schwa planet is that of contamination by outside information, be it a non-Schwa ideological unit, a primitive light-wave transmission from a far-off source, or even the position of the stars in the night sky. An information quarantine is needed to provide the kind of growth medium necessary to maintain Schwa control. The Futureland(TM) template is the latest Schwa-approved information sealant, and this chapter details how to create your very own Futureland(TM) for peace and happiness. Note that the template is designed for use on solid target planets. For gas-giant and liquid worlds, consult Dimensional Archive Item ÷œØ, "Dense-Metal Habitrails: Constraining Input in The Absence of a Solid Crust."

In a glance, the template specifications for Futureland(TM) appear to describe an underground city, but this is too narrow a description. No mere habitation, Futureland(TM) is designed to augment naturally-occurring, Schwa-favorable social patterns and block undesirable idea structures. It does so primarily by using a fair portion of the planet's crust as an insulating layer. The proper architectural arrangement, supplemented by a precision-engineered collective thermostat, is then sufficient to create a biomechanical variable-feedback loop internal to the habitat. For those interested in further reading, the technical specifications are discussed in Dimensional Archive Item @§Ó, "Futureland(TM) Technical Datasheet æÇ´."

The CDI Burrower is included with The Pre-fabricated Futureland(TM) Kit, and The Operator should familiarize itself with its features before proceeding with the underground construction. The Burrower is operated by adaptive artificial intelligence routines designed to minimize non-virtual contact with its controls, but The Operator will have to follow the standard procedures prescribed for all use.

Futureland(TM) itself is merely a question of following the architectural specifications, but there are several points to keep in mind. The Futureland(TM) procedure assumes that molten-rock plumbing has been installed, and that tectonic activity is completely under The Operator's control. Also, while the internal spatial relationships are balanced and the entire system is designed to reward Schwa-friendly activities, the probability of stickpeople boredom still remains high, even with the aggressive use of diversionary programs. It is therefore recommended that The Operator simulate regular natural and artificial disasters, in order to stimulate the mortality-anxiety neural pathways.

ENTER FUTURELAND(TM) HERE

THE FUTURE:
Ⓐ CORPORATE PYRAMID
Ⓑ LANDING CHAMBER
Ⓒ AUTOMATED DEFENSE SYSTEM
Ⓓ XENON STORAGE
Ⓔ DEFENSE SYSTEM MONITORING
Ⓕ BORON ENERGY CHAMBER
Ⓖ CLASSIFIED
Ⓗ MAIN OBSERVATION CHAMBER
Ⓘ EMPLOYMENT
Ⓙ DIVERSION
Ⓚ SEE NEXT PAGE
Ⓛ COLD WATER HEATER
Ⓜ DRAIN

POISON

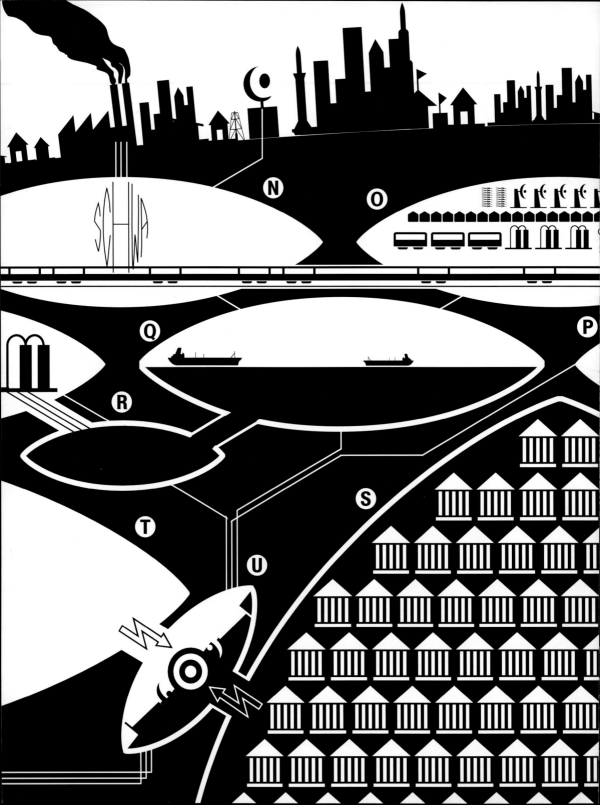

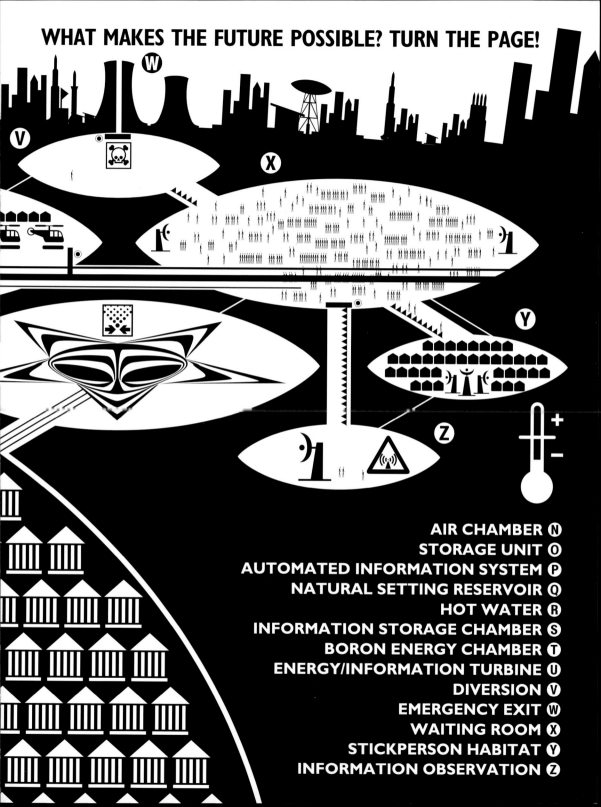

THE NEW CDI BURROWER!

Underground construction is a snap with The Burrower. Outfitted with four blast fusion engines that deliver a combined bore power of over 78,000 megawatts, chasms like the ones shown on the previous pages are carved in just a few hours. That's time saved for more serious activities, and this two-seat automole is definitely the way to get there. Standard equipment includes an internal CCD audio system, super-cooled climate conditioner, and an onboard seismic radar system that lets you know what's going on around you. Six CDI quantum shock pylons give you a smooth and quiet ride rated at 7.5 G's.

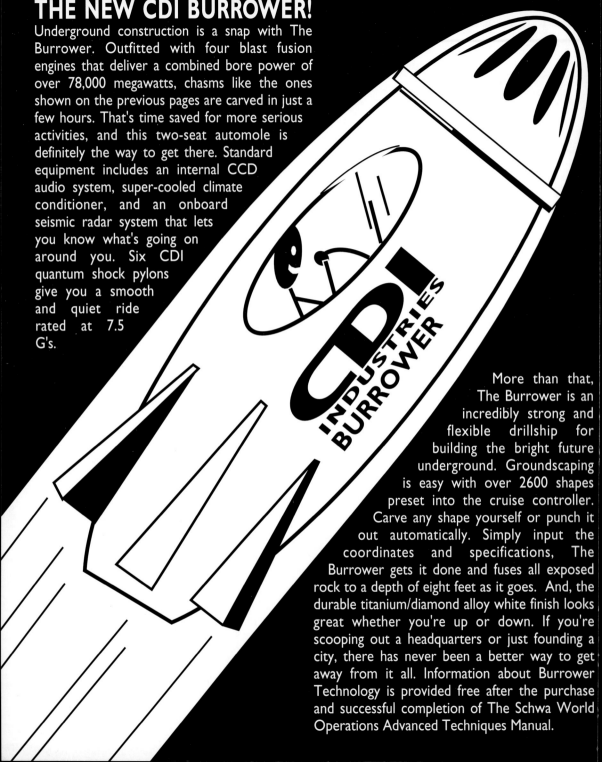

More than that, The Burrower is an incredibly strong and flexible drillship for building the bright future underground. Groundscaping is easy with over 2600 shapes preset into the cruise controller. Carve any shape yourself or punch it out automatically. Simply input the coordinates and specifications, The Burrower gets it done and fuses all exposed rock to a depth of eight feet as it goes. And, the durable titanium/diamond alloy white finish looks great whether you're up or down. If you're scooping out a headquarters or just founding a city, there has never been a better way to get away from it all. Information about Burrower Technology is provided free after the purchase and successful completion of The Schwa World Operations Advanced Techniques Manual.

INTELLECTUALIZE

REFERENCES

INCREDIBLY
FACTUAL

INTELLECTUALIZE-SECTION 12: DIMENSIONS L & 0
ADDITIONAL STUDIES

UTILIZE: How To Gain Control
Atlas of the Dimensions (Schwa Consumer Books, Central AZ, 15-38-46-10: 13,000 pages)
Levy, Marcel. "World Operations" (Ether Publications, Dimension LV, 00-19-96-00)

ACTUALIZE: How To Communicate
Manipulating Business Correspondence (March of Advancement, CDI, 23-07-69-20)

PUBLICIZE: How To Confuse Stickpeople
New Concepts in 26 Dimensions (Old Dominion, Capitol, 30-76-92-30)
Pinnock, Diana. "Practical Stickpeople Herding" (The Eldritch Company, CX, 38-46-15-30)

SERMONIZE: How To Broadcast
Music, Television & Video Handbook (Power Ambition Press, Main City, 82-19-?-?)

ORGANIZE: How To Make Everyone Work
Stickperson Self-Actualization (The Schwa Corporation, N/A: 26 pages)
Gray, Douglas. "Object-Oriented Stickpeople Management" (Vol 78, Issue 65: pages 78-91)
How to Use Flowcharts with Style (The Schwa Corporation, N/A: 3.25 pages)

SUBSIDIZE: How To Acquire Money
Fun With Money! (CDI Printing, °©ƒˇÓ¥ˇØ, 16 86 78 22)

SCHEMATIZE: How To Advance The Plan
Let's Start a Subsidiary! (Technical Support, The Schwa Corporation, N/A)
Subsidiaries And Culpability Insulation (Devious Books, 53-84-61-50: 13 pages)

PERSONALIZE: How To Maintain Success
Studies in Psychography (Psychographic Press, Fractal °¨‰ÂÇˇ, 61-53-84-60)

MAXIMIZE: How To Excel
Exploring The Schwa CogNet! (University of E, Cypher, 69-23-07-60: pages 143-156)
Information Crystallization (Digital Structures, †˜øåœ, 76-92-30-70)

SYMBOLIZE: An Overview
Barker, William. "Schwa & Counter-Schwa" (Qinkos, Dimension R, 19-92-93-94)

METHODIZE: How To Build The Future
Using Your New Burrower! (The Eldritch Company, E Ascending, 84-61-53-80)
Oxereok, Curt, Dr. "Futureland (TM): A Manifesto" (unpublished manuscript)

INTELLECTUALIZE: References
A History of History (Institute of Reality, South X, 92-30-76-90: 28,561 pages)
History Throughout History (Institute of Reality, South X, 07-69-23-00: 26,000 pages)

SPECIALIZE: Appendices
The Theory of Appendice (Desertification of the Mind, Planet E, N/A)

TECHNICAL SUPPORT

Technical support for this version of The World Operations Manual is provided on a time-and-materials basis. A purchase order is required before any service can be authorized. To transition to a contract basis, please contact your dimensional representative. To initiate technical support, use your dimensional index to find your local contact network in Dimensional Archive Item Úf¨. Have a transcription unit ready when you contact Schwa Technical Support, and be near your Schwa Planetary Console if at all possible.

SPECIALIZE

APPENDICES

SUPPORT ALIENOLOGY

INFORMATIONAL COMMANDS:

@A Time/place
@B Weather
@C Planetary Status
@D Disinformation Control
@E Stickpeople Instant Poll
@F Manipulate Resource Allocation

ENTERTAINMENT COMMANDS:

@U Disasters
@V Initiate Tunnel
@W Futureland Controls
@X Release Inhibition Inhibitors
@Y Holiday Generation Controls
@Z Reverse Gravitational Polarity

GLUE ALONG THIS EDGE

THE SCHWA WORLD OPERATIONS MANUAL

TRIM

QUICK REFERENCE PYRAMID ASSEMBLY: To assemble your Quick Reference Pyramid, simply cut along the black-white edges, fold along the dashed lines, place glue along the indicated edge and fasten to the appropriate side. Place next to your Planetary Console for best results. Do not store near volatile or by corrosive liquids.

SECRET STICKPERSON BUTTONS

These buttons are located on the back of your stickpeople's heads in Dimension S. Try various settings and see what happens or press shuffle at random. Record the results.

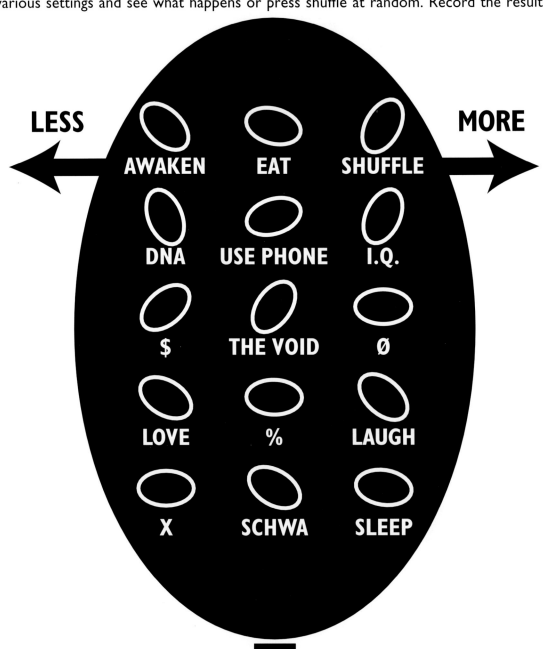

LESS

MORE

AWAKEN   EAT   SHUFFLE

DNA   USE PHONE   I.Q.

$ THE VOID   Ø

LOVE   %   LAUGH

X   SCHWA   SLEEP

26 DIMENSIONAL RULER

This ruler can be used quickly and easily to determine which of the 26 dimensions you are operating in. Follow the simple instructions for assembling the ruler. Use the ruler in any space or against any object. The dimension which is operative at any time or in any place will flash red along with the appropriate letter code, either ascending or descending (for a complete description of the uses of this item see Dimensional Archive Item "'ø^^Å). Warning: Do not put any item through the loop created in the finished ruler as multiple copies of that item are instantly introduced at random to all other inoperative descending dimensions.

THE SCHWA CORPORATION • 26 DIMENSIONS

TRIM

To assemble: Trim the ruler precisely along all four black edges. Firmly grasping both ends of the trimmed ruler, twist ONE of the ends to meet the other end (A to A and Z to Z). While skillfully holding the twisted ruler, tape the now existing seam with clear tape and trim.

SHAPE IS CONCEPT.

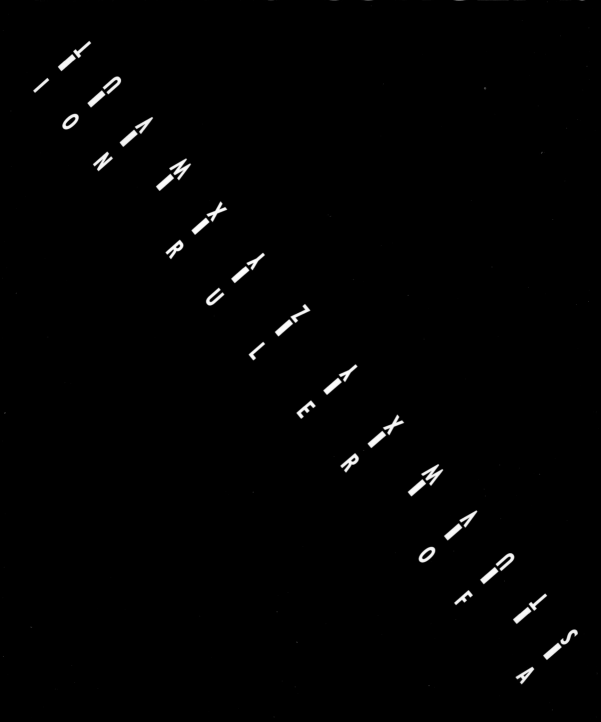

SPECIALIZE-SUBSECTION NM: APPENDIX 4
CEREMONIAL WARRANTY

Thank you for purchasing a Schwa World Operations Manual. In order to protect your new investment, please take a few moments to fill out the warranty registration pages below. Answering the survey questions is not required, but the information will help us to develop a better understanding of you and your personal habits so that we can best meet your needs and ours.

To activate your eternal limited warranty, please copy, complete and mail these pages within 1 day of purchase.

1. Your Title: _____ Other _____

First Name _____ Initials _____

Last Name _____ Nick Name _____

Sector _____ Planet _____ Place _____ Time _____

2. Which media format did you purchase (check one)?
__ Treated Vegetable Pulp __ Magnetic __ Optical __ Schwa BioMem __ Wave __ Other

3. Date of purchase, in Standard XTime Format: _____--_____--_____--_____

4. Serial Number (Dimension N) _____

5. Please check where this product was purchased:
__ Catalog Showroom __ Received as Loan __ Issued by Corporation __ Street Corner

6. Please tell us how you heard about our product:
__ Word-of-Mouth __ Massive Advertising Campaign __ Cryptic Transmission __ Sign
__ Office Memo __ Intuition __ Accusation __ I Didn't

7. Please check the three (3) factors which most influenced your decision to purchase The Schwa World Operations Manual:
__ Style/Appearance __ Peer Pressure __ Sales Representative's Hard-Sell Tactics
__ Price/Value __ Rumor __ Maddening Jingle __ Ignorance __ Confusion

8. Please check the products that you currently own, or intend to purchase in the near future, or would like to imagine owning:

Product	Own	Intend to purchase
Atomic Sex Enhancer	____	____
Psychic Pain Remover	____	____
Schwa Car	____	____
Alien Brand(TM) Computer	____	____
Technical Support Manual	____	____
Schwa Planet Kit	____	____
The Schwa Corporation	____	____

9. How did you pay for your **World Operations Manual?**

__ Cash __ Check __ Metal __ Schwa Credit Card __ Stickpeople __ Other Commodities

10. Occupation:

	You	Your Life Partner
Secret	___	___
Politician	___	___
Inventor	___	___
Clerical	___	___
Social Director	___	___
Thinker	___	___
Eccentric Billionaire	___	___
Unoccupied	___	___

11. To help us completely understand our customers' lifestyles, please indicate the interests and activities in which you and your friends enjoy participating on a regular basis:

Activity/Interest	You	Your Friends
Conspiring	___	___
Driving	___	___
Running	___	___
Scanning Night Skies	___	___
Gardening	___	___
Talking Superficially	___	___
Collectibles/Collections	___	___
Controlling Others	___	___
Fixing Computers	___	___
Household Pets	___	___
Reading Satire	___	___

12. Salutation: Thanks for taking the time to fill out this questionnaire. Your answers will be used in market studies that will help Schwa serve you better in the future, as well as allowing you to receive mailings and special offers from other companies, fringe groups, and mysterious phenomena.

13. Comments or suggestions about our products? Please contact:

The Schwa Corporation
Customer Service Department
Section μø°, Appendice Division
Dimension B, Level 39
Room 4,826,809

SCHWA ®

CERTIFICATE OF COMPLETION

WORLD OPERATIONS MANUAL

This document indicates that _____ has passed the required testing to reach the Termination of Training, and is fully qualified to operate as a Planet Operator. This document should not be taken as an admission of liability by Schwa or its subsidiaries.* For more information about this document, consult The Schwa Corporation's Legal Document çⓒß˜78, "Rights, Responsibilities and Regulations Attached to Certificates of Completion."

SUPERVISOR: _____

WITNESS: _____

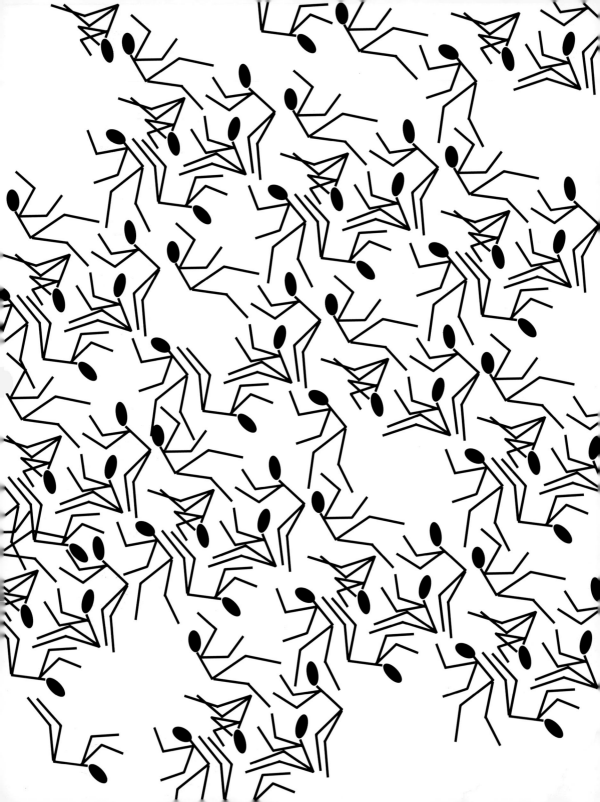

NOTES, SKETCHES AND QUESTIONS